W9-AFC-509

Gramley Library
Salem College
Winston-Salem, NC 27108

THE QUEST OF THE BALLAD

In this retreat the stories of yesterday are developed today.

77537

PR
9180
.M3
1966

THE QUEST OF THE BALLAD

BY

W. ROY MACKENZIE

PROFESSOR OF ENGLISH, WASHINGTON UNIVERSITY

HASKELL HOUSE
Publishers of Scholarly Books
NEW YORK
1966

SALEM COLLEGE LIBRARY
WINSTON-SALEM, N. C.

published by

HASKELL HOUSE

Publishers of Scholarly Books

30 East 10th Street • New York, N. Y. 10003

PRINTED IN UNITED STATES OF AMERICA

PREFACE

There used to be a literary affectation—a harmless and quite transparent one—which expressed itself in a prefatory announcement that one's book had been written, not for an astute and difficult public, but for one's own private solace and the amusement of one's small and charitable circle of friends. Though I have no intention of taking sanctuary in this timid pretext I have nevertheless a vehement realization, induced by the disquieting experience of reading the proof-sheets of the ensuing book, that I must fashion some explanation that will seem to account for a conspicuous absence of plan. The truth is that my initial purpose was, not to write a book, but merely to reproduce, for any purpose that might ultimately be served, a few of my successive adventures with the ancient singers of ballads whose society I have eagerly courted during my summer vacations in Nova Scotia. The chapters, then, in which I follow a dim trail of chronological sequence are the expression of my first complete intention. But the popular ballad, even when it is pursued through printed collections and song-books, impresses one in many ways by virtue of its variable and elusive personality, and when its character is further enriched by a continued association with its natural companions, the singers, he would be dull indeed of soul who could pass it by without attempting to capture something of the secret of its habits. As a matter of fact I had not yet completed my brief chronological sequence of chapters before I had become interested in the questions which have led to the topical discussions of the later chapters. These questions I have taken up in the order in which they have occurred to me. After the fifth

vii

77537

chapter I give one faint sign, and one only, of my latent regard for order, and that is the scarcely avoidable act of placing a picture of the decline of ballad-singing at the end of the book. But I must not utterly deny myself the right to that guerdon of praise which is so earnestly desired by every man who writes for publication. My constant purpose has been to portray, as faithfully as in me lies, the popular ballads which it has been my high privilege to encounter in their natural state and the reserved but simple and profoundly human old men and women who are still maintaining them in that state. It is this purpose that is responsible for the inconsistency of my plan, and though the reader may esteem consistency a jewel he must needs agree that my purpose was a commendable one.

The person who sets out in these latter days to collect and preserve the scattered ballads that are still living upon the earth must prepare to search wide and far, and must make sure that he is not easily to be discouraged. Even in communities where ballads are occasionally sung they are rarely known to the children of the present generation; nor need one turn hopefully to the fathers, for the cares of this world and the deceitfulness of riches have in a practical age grown up in their minds and killed the good seed of the ballads which was lightly sown there in the days of their youth; but with a somewhat larger prospect of success one may seek out and question the grandfathers, if haply they have survived to a day which has provided so many duties and amusements to supplant the simple recreations of a bygone age. I speak out of my own almost uniform experience, and the persons who appear and reappear in the following pages are, with the fewest exceptions, men and women of three-score years and upwards. My collecting, to be sure, has all been done in Nova Scotia, and the situation there is not necessarily typical in all of its details. There are still some districts where ballads are sung by children, but they are far removed from the world, and the children are not children of the twentieth century.

My motive in writing this introduction is the conventionally double one—to confess with an ostentatious humility the obvious defects in the book to follow, and to commend, with an equally ostentatious moderation, its merits. I shall now proceed to the second phase. My book is almost free from taint of theory, and in its pages darkness is not rendered visible by any attempt of mine to solve the ballad problem. This is a negative cause for pride. The positive and authentic cause of which I boast is the admittance which has repeatedly been granted me to the companionship of a class of human beings almost unknown and now swiftly disappearing from society. It is with this companionship and its fruits that I am solely concerned, and the pride which I have confessed is abated only when I compare my recollections with the pictures of them which have issued from my pen.

In my first chapters I insist with a good deal of solemn unction upon the difficulty of persuading the ballad-singer to open his door. But the comfort of the fireside is only enhanced for him who has first cooled his heels upon the doorstep, and in the chiaroscuro of my ballad-seeking memories the element of toil and hazard serves chiefly to accentuate my ensuing delight in the substantial reward of fresh ballads to add to the growing tale. The grossest impediment in the whole enterprise, probably, is the mechanical task of writing down ballads at lightning speed. The singer can rarely repeat his song slowly enough to permit one to write at a normal rate, and if I were to begin the canvassing of another district I should be compelled to recognize the advisability of forcing myself to the hideous preliminary task of mastering the science of shorthand.

But even while driving my fingers to the benumbing labour of copying sixty words to the minute I have many times experienced a swelling of the bosom at the loud admiration that I was evoking by my chirographic skill, a gift most lightly valued and utterly undistinguished in the community of reading and writing moderns which I inhabit during the nine months of the college year. There comes into my mind at this moment a recollection of one afternoon when I was tearing along over the blank sheets in a frenzied endeavor to keep pace with an old man who could repeat his ballads only if he kept his eyes tightly closed and proceeded without a single pause. His wife and her gossip from the next farmhouse sat by, and while I accomplished herculean tasks with my pen they regarded me with undisguised wonder and delight. "Will ye look at that man writin'!" cried the goodwife. "He's settin' there as easy and comfortable as if he was eatin' he's dinner, an' see the way them songs is bein' writ down!"

"Yes, yes," interrupted the neighbour with shrill ecstacy, "he jist sets there smokin' he's pipe, an', O Lord, but aint he drivin' he's fingers over that paper!"

> I once did hold it, as our statists do,
> A baseness to write fair, and labour'd much
> How to forget that learning, but, sir, now
> It did me yeoman's service.

I shall presently be charged with having acquired from my ancient companions the senile habit of garrulity. In truth, I find that I have little to say by way of preface that I could not say with equal propriety in any of the chapters of my rambling book—with one important exception, which is this. I should never have had the persistence to keep my work going but for the aid and good cheer of my coadjutors, and of these I shall mention three, though I

can afford them only the smallest return for their services
by a meagre prefatory acknowledgment. From the beginning of my labours my wife has had a far greater interest in the work and a far greater faith in the ballad-
yielding possibilities of Nova Scotia than I have had.
Many a time I should have allowed the whole matter to
lapse but for her contagious enthusiasm and her practical
aid in placating suspicious persons who would never have
sung unless they had felt inclined to do so although the
heavens had threatened to fall. My cousin, Dr. Owen
Cameron, has also accompanied me on innumerable journeys to the huts where poor men lie. In my narration of
these journeys I have striven to direct attention steadily
upon the singers and have almost uniformly designated
the visiting party by the colorless and half impersonal pro-
noun "I", but the reader may substitute "the doctor and
I" as often as he chooses. Many of the finest ballads that
I quote and many of the singers to whose rich personali-
ties I do such scanty justice would never have appeared in
my pages at all without his help. And my aider and abet-
tor in everything that I have done in the service of the
popular ballad has been Professor Kittredge. In my
student days he infected me with something of his own
broadly human interest in folk-lore, he showed such generous enthusiasm over my first scanty "finds" that I was
forthwith emboldened to look for more, and he persuaded
me to attempt my first brief essays in describing my experiences. If my "little book" of reminiscences is of interest to these and to my other coadjutors it shall not fail
to justify itself in my sight.

August, 1919.   W. R. M.

CONTENTS

CHAPTER ONE

The Last Refuge of the Ballad

The persons faintly shadowed forth in this record are of a type which has long been absent from the places where the business of the world is transacted, and which is now disappearing from the face of the earth itself. Each year brings its increase of scholars and students to whom popular lore is a vital record of the beliefs of their forefathers, but the years produce few people in our time who accept as credible reports the tales and songs which scholars designate, somewhat condescendingly, as "folk-lore." It is gradually becoming impossible for the individual to remain unaffected by the main current of events. The countryside has been brought to the gates of the town, and the newspaper which appears on the breakfast-table of the urban tradesman has travelled by noon to the shepherd's cot and the fisherman's hut. Now, it is axiomatic that he who reads the newspaper shall cease to be a perpetuator of folk-lore. The *sine qua non* of the latter, in our time at least, is an aloofness from the world of progress, a mellow retirement where the events of a bygone day are rather more near and familiar than are the noises of the great city which is understood to be flourishing in its iniquity somewhere far beyond the possibilities of man's travel. In this retreat the stories of yesterday are developed today, and are not dispossessed by a set of new sensations freshly imported by the morning paper. And even those accounts which filter in from the great world

1

are distilled through the limbeck of the oral report until they take on something of the true nature of traditional legend. Let me give a brief example or two, modern instances of the way in which history was fashioned for our ancestors in the dim ages.

In one of the sequestered vales of Nova Scotia there is living at the present time an ancient sage by the name of Peter Langille. His age is ninety-two, his habits of body and mind are active and vigorous, and his tongue is endowed with the gift of a simple and picturesque eloquence. In his youth and prime he followed the sea, or rather the sea-coast, in one of the little schooners that used to ply their busy trade along the northern shores of Nova Scotia. Now in his green old age he goes fishing when the fishing is good, and when it is not he reposes in dignified ease by his fireside or in his dooryard, where he may usually be found having a crack with one of the neighbors or pondering alone upon the riddle of the painful earth. He is one of my friends and, in the brief glimpses of the summer vacation, one of my associates.

One forenoon in the early days of the great war I walked over to Peter's cottage and inquired after the news. "De British," stated Peter with great calmness, "has won a tremendious victory over de Garmans." I was eager for details of the combat, but Peter was not to be rushed. "Set down," he said, "an' fill yer pipe, an' I'll give ye de pertickilars." Then, after I had loaded my pipe and settled my chair against the wall, he resumed. "De victory," he explained, "was won by an old Scotch gineral. He was at de head of five hunderd men, all wit' dere guns loaded an' lined up waitin' for de Garmans to come on. 'Now,' sez he to he's men, 'I wants ye all to stay quiet jist

2

as I've drawed ye up, an' don't ye dar to fire a gun till I gives ye de word.' Purty soon de Garmans hove in sight an' come ragin' along firin' off dere guns as fast as dey could load dem. 'Keep still, boys,' sez de old gineral, 'till I gives ye de word.' So dey laid low till de Garmans gits wit'in good range, an' den de old gineral ups an' yells: 'Now, boys, up wit' yer guns an' fire at dem!' Bang goes dere guns, every one o' dem at onct, an, oh God, but didn't dey slaughter dem Garmans! Five t'ousand o' dem went down, an' de ones dat was left hove away dere guns an' made fer de woods."

To an American reader this stirring report will sound like a foolish bit of fiction stimulated by patriotic fervor in the mind of an illiterate countryman, a tale full of sound and fury, signifying nothing; but to the Canadian who is mindful of the early pages in his country's history it will mean something more. There are certain chapters in the political history of every country that are known only to the esoteric circle of readers, but the great military exploits of a nation are familiar, in one form or another, to every member of that nation. In Canada it is only the student of affairs who can give you the story of Federation, but every peasant there has his version of the battle on the plains of Abraham, the great fight in which General Wolfe wrested the key of Canada from the French leader Montcalm and paid the price of victory with his life. A popular ballad tells us that

> Brave Wolfe drew up his men
> In a line so pritty
> On the Plains of Abraham
> Before the city.

And in my own childhood I have heard an old ship-carpenter narrate the glowing tale, which he thus introduced: "Gineral Wolfe climbed de trecipice, camped on de Plains of Abraham, an' prayed for night or Blutcher to come."

It must not be supposed that I have forgotten old Peter, who is sitting patiently by his kitchen stove smoking his pipe and musing on the prowess and skill of the British soldiers at the front. I am merely evolving a pedantic explanation of Peter's remarkable report of the battle, and my explanation is this: A story of success to the British arms had been reported in the community, and in the popular consciousness undisturbed by alphabetical symbols the report had taken on the outlines of a great British victory long celebrated in song and legend. The "old Scotch gineral," in short, had done exactly what Wolfe had done when he drew up his men to face the oncoming battalions of the French under Montcalm.

In this simple tale we have an illustration of the whole progress of folk-lore. The reports of the present are fashioned in the mould of popular history, and there is no recourse, as in the learned world, to the sanctified authority of the printed document. The great composite of fact and legend wrought by the ballad-maker and the popular historian has been produced in divers ways, and in its mingled warp and woof there are strands brought from many far countries. No student of folk-lore need be reminded, for instance, that the popular ballads frequently present unauthorized versions of the tales of Holy Writ, and in Nova Scotia Biblical history often escapes from the Calvinistic fold and wanders in curious garments among untutored folk who receive their tales only through the true popular medium of oral transmission. In such cases it comports itself in a way that would be quite new and strange to anyone who is imperfectly acquainted with the processes of legend.

There comes to my mind a memory of one rainy afternoon that I spent in the lonely cabin of "Little Eph," which is the affectionate nickname employed in Tatamagouche to designate old Ephraim Tattrie. Little Eph was valiantly combating the gloom of the outer world by singing shanties, ballads, and other "songs of good life," and one of them was "The Battle of Alma."

Come all you Britons, I pray give ear
To these few lines I've brought you here,
To these few lines I've brought you here,
    The victory gained at Alma.

Cho. Sing tantinaray ri til di day
      Sing tantinaray ri til di day
      To these few lines I've brought you here,
        The victory gained at Alma.

It was on September the twentieth day,
In spite of all salt dash and spray
We landed safe on the Crimay
    All on the route for Alma.

Cho. Sing tantinaray, etc.

All night we lay on the cold ground,
No shade or shelter to be found,
And while with rain we were almost drowned
    To cheer our hearts for Alma.

Cho. Sing tantinaray, etc.

5

Next morning a burning sun did rise
Beneath the eastern cloudless skies,
When our great chief Lord Raglan cries,
   "Prepare your march for Alma."

Cho.   Sing tantinaray, etc.

When Alma's heights did heave in view
The stoutest hearts it would subdue
To see the Rooshians' monstrous crew
   On the towering heights of Alma.

Cho.   Sing tantinaray, etc.

But when the heights we did command
We boldly fought them hand to hand,
The Rooshians could no longer stand
   Our British charge at Alma.

Cho.   Sing tantinaray, etc.

The Rooshians to Sebastopol fled
Leaving their wounded and their dead,
They thought next day the river run red
   With the blood was spilt at Alma.

Cho.   Sing tantinaray, etc.

The English I have heard them say
They lost ten thousand men that day,
While thirteen thousand Frenchmen lay
   In their bloody gore at Alma.

Cho.   Sing tantinaray, etc.

This song is a pæan of triumph, an exultant ode rather than a plain narrative of the fight, and Little Eph quite properly felt that it devolved upon him to furnish more stark details than the song by itself afforded. "I'll tell ye," he explained, "how dat great victory over de Rooshians was gained. King William was leadin' de English, an' along about de end of de afternoon dey had de Rooshians purty near licked, but not quite, an' jist den de sun started to set. Down went King William on he's knees an' prayed to God to hold de sun still fer a little while longer. Den he jumped onto he's feet an' grabbed he's sword and went at dem, an' God held de sun where it was till de Rooshians was well licked an' on de run like a drove of sheep. An' as soon as de fight was over de sun went down."

A few pages back I felt constrained to offer a scientific explanation of old Peter Langille's report of the battle "somewhere in France," but that was because the actual background of Peter's account was a bit of history which is the common possession of Canadians rather than of Americans. As a teacher of English literature I have learned that one must not lightly assume that those who read books have a common background of Biblical lore, and I have therefore some reason to suspect that I should render Little Eph's tale more luminous by the addition of a marginal gloss; but I shall pay my readers the compliment of taking it for granted that to do so would be quite superfluous, and if I make it necessary for a chance reader to look up his reference for Eph's exposition I shall at least be doing him no harm.

These brief excerpts from the conversations of Peter and of Eph are merely random illustrations of the point of view constantly maintained by the persons who sing popular ballads and to whom superstition and legend are

7

as the morning newspaper is to their more progressive fellow-creatures. Such persons are now exceedingly rare, and, as though they realized their value in a world which is soon to lose them altogether, they often make themselves most difficult of access, but they are nowadays the only true possessors of that precious gift handed down from ancient times, the song and story of the unlettered and imaginative folk. Behind the shelter of their closed doors they sing popular ballads which disappeared from public view many years ago, and which in many cases have come down to them through centuries of singing and recitation.

My childhood was spent in a district which, as I now know, was a rich unworked mine of English and Scottish popular ballads. By laboring intermittently in this district for the last six or seven years I have painfully gathered a collection which is to me more precious than much fine gold; but the specimens in this collection have been found by minute search in strange and secluded places, by exploring the depths of the forest and descending into the caves of the ocean. Of the people who live in the various communities that I have ransacked, the great majority have neither heard of these ballads nor have ever suspected the hidden powers of the persons who sang them for me.

In my youthful days there was one ballad which, by a sort of accident, emerged from the secret places where ballads were lurking, and which was captured and exhibited in civilized quarters as a vastly amusing curiosity. This was "The Butcher Boy," a song which by virtue of its lugubrious handling of a pathetic tale made a special appeal to nurse-maids, scullery-wenches, and sentimental ship-carpenters. But this species of popularity would never have raised it from the subliminal region. The process was accomplished in a much more effective way. A humble but resourceful man of ease taught it to his small son and basely instigated the latter to prostitute the ancient practice of minstrelsy by singing it to anyone who would give him a penny for the performance. The lad so lustily advertised his commodity that it soon became a regular amusement in the village to traffic with him on the street corners, and many persons who knew nothing and cared as much about ballads learned this one and repeated it as a fine bit of unconscious humor. I have recently copied it down from the singing of one who regarded it with seriousness, and shall now present it in order to illustrate the sort of qualities that cause the ballad to be regarded with merriment in civilized communities. Those who read it will be inclined to laugh rather than to weep, and will thus, perhaps, be able to understand the reticence of the present-day singer who loves and honors his ballads.

> In London town, where I did dwell,
> A butcher boy I loved him well.
> He courted me for many a day,
> He stole from me my heart away.
>
> I mind the time, not long ago,
> He'd follow me through frost and snow.
> But now he's changed his mind again.
> He'll pass my door and he won't come in.
>
> There is an inn in that same town,
> And there my love he sits him down.
> He takes a strange girl on his knee,
> And tells her what he once told me.

But I can tell you the reason why:
Because she's got more gold than I.
But gold will melt and silver fly.
She'll see the day as poor as I.

I'll go upstairs and make my bed.
"There is nothing to do," my mother said.
My mother she has followed me,
Saying, "What is the matter, my daughter dear?"

Oh mother dear, you little know
What pains or sorrow or what woe.
So get a chair and sit me down.
With pen and ink I'll write all down.

She wrote a letter, she wrote a song.
She wrote a letter, she wrote it long.
On every line she dropped a tear,
At every verse cried, "Willie dear!"

Her father he came home that night
Enquiring for his heart's delight.
He went upstairs, the door he broke.
He found her hanging on a rope.

He took a knife and cut her down,
And in her bosom these lines he found:
"Oh what a foolish girl was I
To hang myself for a butcher boy.

"Go dig my grave both wide and deep.
Put a marble stone at my head and feet.
And on my grave place a turtle dove,
To show the world that I died of love."

10

It is hardly necessary to insist that this ballad was composed with the utmost seriousness and with the most complete sympathy for the poor maid whose affections were basely trifled with by the thoughtless and debonair butcher boy. Furthermore, it was composed for persons who would take a precisely similar view of the case, and who would agree with the composer or composers in feeling that the language employed for the setting forth of the tragedy was fitting and dignified. Presently, however, it falls into the hands of people who see something inherently comic in the spectacle of a girl bewailing the perfidy of a mere butcher's apprentice, and who have read magazines, newspapers, and other refined forms of literature sufficiently to conclude that the language of the ballad is quaint, old-fashioned, and absurdly naïve. Small wonder, then, if the few people who know this ballad and others equally old-fashioned, and who regard them with real affection and esteem, should be extremely chary about subjecting them to the merriment of unsympathetic strangers in the outer world.

If I had been born fifty years earlier I might have seen many a ballad flaunting itself bravely in the public haunts of men. In my time, however, and out of the scores of old songs that I have discovered in one way or another, "The Butcher Boy" is the only one that has thus ventured out of its hiding-place; and it, as we have seen, was betrayed and sold by one who, according to the unwritten code of the ballad-singer, should have constituted himself its guardian and protector. The singer himself rarely takes the pains to inquire into the causes lying back of his determined reticence. He knows that in the old days he was applauded and envied for his dramatic power to arouse pity

11

SALEM COLLEGE LIBRARY
WINSTON-SALEM, N. C.

and terror by his singing, and he has seen in later days the indifference and the occasional merriment which have succeeded the strong old emotions. These are stark facts which in recent years have forced themselves upon him with a cruel insistence, and he seldom asks for an explanation, though the explanation is not far to seek.

It is a very obvious truth that simple amusements can be honestly appraised only by the simple. Those of us who are sophisticated may be heartily entertained by such amusements, but we cannot accept them in the spirit of the persons for whom they were originally planned. We are in entire accord with the spirit of Stevenson's "Child's Garden of Verses," composed by an educated and experienced person who loved and understood children, and who adopted the language, not of the child, but of the loving parent or friend who is for the moment striving to put himself into the child's frame of mind. When the child himself turns his hand to verse, we look upon the result with merriment, derision, or tenderness, as the case may be, but always with a distinct sense of our own superiority. And precisely similar is our attitude towards the popular ballad. We laugh at the "quaint language" in which the forlorn maiden expresses her sorrow for the loss of her beloved butcher boy, instead of feeling that this would be a very beautiful way for us to express our emotions if we were placed in the same tragic situation. For this, obviously enough, we sophisticated persons are not to be blamed, any more than is the ballad-singer when he senses the superiority in our bearing and refuses to expose to our possible merriment the songs which he loves and honors.

I am, of course, speaking in a general way of the up-to-date, newspaper-reading world and its comfortable sense

12

of superiority. In that world there are many nominal residents, like myself, who have developed for the old tales and songs of the folk a love which in its way is no less genuine than that of the few survivors of the folk themselves. We are, to be sure, strongly influenced by our knowledge of the literature that has been produced in our more conventional world, and constantly apply to the poetry of the folk a sort of criticism that would never occur to the composers or singers themselves. But, on the other hand, we have the advantage of being able to view this poetry in the light—though it is often a very dim one— of the historical or social atmosphere in which it was actually composed, whereas the singer himself, if his ballad has come from the distant past, can attach his interest only to its intrinsic qualities.

But this plea that I am making for myself as a genuine lover of popular ballads is not one that would admit me to the confidence of the ballad-singer. It is necessary that I should convince him in a much more simple and human fashion that he has found in me a person with old-fashioned tastes and enthusiasms. The difficulties of the ballad-collector have their rise in the task of discovering a potential singer, and they have their continuance in the task of persuading him, when he is discovered, to reveal his art to one who is in outward appearance only a supercilious visitor from the conventional world; and thus it devolves upon the collector to utilize all his gifts of cunning and persuasion upon the slightest suspicion that he may be in the neighborhood of a concealed ballad. In my own collection of "goodly songs and ballets" the one that I view with the greatest pride is a composite version of the old ballad of "Little Musgrave." Under the title of "Lit-

13

tle Matha Grove" it had been sung to me, when I was a lad, by an old man in the neighborhood where I have since been working as a collector. But when I began my search for ballads my old friend had transferred his art, as I hope, to a higher sphere of musical endeavor, and for many months my strictest inquiries failed to produce another singer who could repeat the performance. I shall have occasion later to tell the story of my discovery of "Little Matha Grove," but the fact is that, at the time of my search, there were at least three persons in the community who could, in a more or less defective fashion, sing this rare old ballad. The composite version I shall now quote in full as a prize specimen of the treasures of folk-lore that lie, hidden and guarded, in the memories of the few survivors of the old singing days.

> 'Twas on a day, a high holiday,
>   The best day of the old year,
> When little Matha Grove he went to church
>   The holy word to hear.
>
> Some came in in diamonds of gold,
>   And some came in in pearls,
> And among them all was little Matha Grove
>   The handsomest of them all.
>
> Lord Daniel's wife who was standing by,
>   On him she cast her eye,
> Saying, "This very night, you little Matha
>   Grove,
>   You must come with me and lie."
>
> "I wouldn't for the world, I wouldn't for my
>   life,

14

For fear Lord Daniel should hear.
For I know you are Lord Daniel's wife
  By the ring on your hand you do wear."

"Well, what if I am Lord Daniel's wife
  As you suppose me to be?
Lord Daniel's away to the New Castle
  King Henry for to see."

So the little foot-page was standing by,
  And he heard all that was said,
And he took to his heels to the river-side,
  And he bended his breast and he swum.

And when he came to Lord Daniel's bower,
  He knocked so hard at the ring.
There was none so ready as Lord Daniel
  For to rise and let him in.

"What news, what news, my little foot-page,
  Do you bring unto me?"
"This very night little Matha Grove
  Is in bed with your wedded lady."

"If this be true, be true unto me,
  Be true you bring unto me,
I have an only daughter dear,
  And your wedded lady she shall be.

"If this be a lie, a lie unto me,
  A lie you bring unto me,
I'll cause a gallows to be rigged,
  And hangèd you shall be."

15

So he put the bugle to his mouth,
  And he sounded loud and shrill:
"If there's any man in bed with another man's
    wife,
  It is time to be hastening away."

So Lord Daniel he ordered up all his men,
  And he placed them in a row.

.   .   .   .

    .   .   .   .   .   .

"What's that, what's that?" said little Matha
    Grove,
  "For I know the sound so well.
It must be the sound of Lord Daniel's bugle,"

.   .   .   .   .   .

"Lie still, lie still, you little Matha Grove,
  And keep me from the cold.
It's only my father's shepherd boy
  That's driving sheep down in the fold."

So they hustled and they tumbled till they both
    fell asleep,
  And nothing more did they say
Till Lord Daniel stood by their bedside
  Little Matha for to slay.

"How do you like my bed?" said he,
  "And how do you like my sheet?
And how do you like my wedded lady
  That lies in your arms and sleeps?"

"Well do I like your bed," said he,
  "Well do I like your sheet.
Better do I like your wedded lady,
  That lies in my arms and sleeps."

16

"Get up, get up, you little Matha Grove,
  And some of your clothes put on,
That it can't be said after your death
  That I slew a naked man."

"How can I get up," little Matha replied,
  "And fight you for my life,
When you have two bright swords by your
    side,
  And I have ne'er a knife?"

"If I have two bright swords by my side,
  They cost me deep in purse,
And you shall have the best of them,
  And I shall have the worst.

"And you shall have the very first blow,
  And I shall have the other.
What more, then, could I do for you
  If you were my own born brother?"

The very first blow that Matha Grove struck
  He wounded Lord Daniel sore.
The very first blow Lord Daniel struck,
  Little Matha could strike no more.

"Cursèd be my wife!" said he,
  "And cursèd be my hand!
They have caused me to slay the prettiest lad
  That ever trod England's land."

He took his lady by the hand,
  He led her through the plain,
And he never spoke another word
  Till he split her head in twain.

17

He put his sword against the ground,
  The point against his heart.
There never was three lovers
  That sooner did depart.

While it is still possible to find such ballads as this in the possession of humble folk who shall say that the ballad collector's function is a barren one? He will have to search far and wide if he is to find many such relics as the one I have just shown, for as surely as the good knight's sword has turned to rust so surely is the popular singing of ballads ceasing to be heard in the land. But as this ancient custom approaches its dissolution the more need is there that one should hasten to record something of its operation, for when the singers and historians of the folk disappear, as they presently will, we shall have left only a few printed versions of their lore, dry bones from that great body of song and story that once lived and moved among forgotten people of the earth.

CHAPTER TWO

The Way of the Collector

I wish to proceed, as soon as I conveniently can, to a rough narrative account of my first experiences with ballad-singing folk. This account will lead me back in memory to the time—six or seven years ago—when I set out to recover, if possible, some versions of the ancient Scotch ballads which I had heard when I was a boy, and which were freshly brought to my mind in my college days by a study of Professor Child's collection. Though the path which I trod in those first years of my quest was beset with shards and flint, in the retrospect it seems fair and flowery, and retrospect will inevitably play its mollifying part in my narrative. Therefore I deem it just to bend my attention for a moment to a deliberate recognition of the difficulties of ballad collecting, and, in the sacred interests of verisimilitude, to insert a preliminary chapter which shall expound and illustrate some of the trials which any honest collector must prepare to meet—and to overcome.

The situation, then, that faces the would-be collector of popular ballads is one that, if it tempt him at all, must tempt him by reason of its abundant opportunities for developing his faculties of ingenuity and persistence. He must bravely accept the two main discouraging facts, first, that only in the rarest cases do ballads still exist as a popular tradition, and, secondly, that the few old men and women who are familiar with them are excessively unwilling to reveal this familiarity to anyone but a trusted friend

19

or relative. The rude winds of neglect, scorn, and contumely have so chilled the custom that its few loyal adherents instinctively feel that it is for them to give it protection and warmth at their own hearths, and to bar the door against the blasts from the outer world, which may bring inquisitive strangers who desire to hear ballads sung in order to hold them up to ridicule.

The worst possible manner in which to begin the siege of a potential singer would be to approach, salute, and make known the object of the visit,—namely, to procure old songs. The ardent lover might just as well begin his courtship by a downright proposal for the hand of his mistress. By this bold stroke the lover might conceivably have his hopes crowned on the instant, but he would be much more likely to prolong his courtship by several months, or even to render its continuance inadvisable. And no bashful maid was ever more coy or more elusive than is the hoary-headed vendor of outworn ballads. Any display of impetuosity on the part of the collector would immediately lay him under the suspicion of being a seeker after that sort of pleasure which is stimulated by the spectacle of a fellow-creature making a fool of himself. He would be reproved,—and even when exhibiting the most punctilious deportment he frequently is reproved,—by the searching question, "So ye just thought ye'd come around to have a little fun with me, did ye?"

The collector, then, who keeps his eye on the ultimate goal will realize that he must take his time and cover his ground before he can hope to reach that goal. He will open the conversation by discoursing gravely on topics judiciously selected from the five following classes: weather, crops, sickness, politics, and religion. Thus he will convey the impression that he is a civil, trustworthy person, and not a mere thoughtless tormentor of the old and venerable. After this impression is driven home the collector will guide his sober conversation towards a series of reflections upon the songs of the present and those of the past, in which he will voice his conviction that the old is better than the new, and avow that, as for him, his tastes are of the old-fashioned sort. Then he may, with what skill Heaven has given him, let slip the question which he has been holding in the leash; and he will, if my experiences are typical, receive some such response as this: "Ah, God bless me, I might a' been able to sing one or two o' them old songs once, but it's manys a long year now sence I've thought o' them. The only man around these parts that would likely mind of any songs now is old John Kennedy, an' if ye drive straight along the road for two miles, an' then turn to yer right down the shore road ye'll come to where he lives." Whereupon I should neither drive two miles along the road nor yet turn to my right down the shore road, but should remain in my seat and by degrees extract from my inside pocket a lead-pencil and a writing-pad, preparing to use the same on the strength of the understatement just received. This process is given as an imaginary one, but it is the reflection of many an actual encounter in which I have borne a part.

The labor, then, of collecting ballads is arduous and often extremely discouraging; but in some few cases the reward of honest endeavor is immediate and complete. One September afternoon I drove six miles in a pelting storm to interview a certain old, savage, man-eating tiger in the shape of a north-shore fisherman by the name of Sandy Macdonald. As I entered the kitchen Sandy recognized me from his seat behind the stove. "Ah yes," he bellowed, "you're the professor, ain't ye? My God, man, but ye must be rich!" I responded with the cautious moderation which, I think, should always be assumed by men of my profession when they discuss personal affairs of this sort, but Sandy was not to be shaken from his position. His emphatic conclusion was, "Ye must be buildin' up a great fortune." In the elevation of spirit brought on by this heartening assurance I was moved to remark unto Sandy that when travelling in the rain I frequently carried a pocket-vessel containing a well-known Scottish restorative, as an antidote to the grosser forms of dampness. My information elicited another stentorian avowal, and this time I could not reasonably dissent. "Ha!" roared my host, "and, by the Lord, ye're a gentleman too!—Sit down," he added, "and I'll do what I can for ye." Sandy did not have many ballads at his command, but of such as he had he gave freely.

But I must on no account allow myself to be seduced by the pleasant recollection of this happy experience into leaving the impression that it is typical. Occasionally one may tread the straight path into the confidence of a singer to whom the creature comforts of life are dear, and only a few months ago I spent an afternoon with a jolly old dog who, within fifteen minutes after I had greeted him, expressed profound regret that he had so little to offer me in return for my well-placed friendliness. But ease is by no means the rule; and in the case of singers who take their art seriously, recollecting that in their youth they were profoundly respected as dignified entertainers of the community, the wall of reserve is likely to have become high and hard to climb. These are the singers who, as a rule, possess the ballads which the collector is most eager to obtain, and they will display them only to that person who can persuade them that, in a cynical age, he really feels the respectful admiration which animated the circle of listeners in the good old days.

During the years of my sporadic endeavor in the ballad field I have run a good part of what I conceive to be the gamut of the collector's experience. I have returned home at evening laden with spoils which were procured as easily as though Heaven had showered them, manna-like, upon the ground before me, and I have toiled for days on end with no other reward than the final discovery that I was operating upon barren soil. By way of a brief illustration, I shall now narrate the adventure of a day which is fairly typical of the life of him who follows the dim trail of the surviving English and Scotch ballads.

On a smoking hot July afternoon, some years ago, I drove ten or twelve miles over a narrow, dusty road in search of an old Scotch Canadian named Thomas Mc-Farlane. Old Thomas had been described to me as an eccentric person of outworn habits who could frequently be heard chanting strange music in a minor key while performing his daily chores, and my informer had deduced the entirely false inference that he would prove to be the sort of singer that I delighted to honor. Buoyed up, then, with lying hopes and expectations, I drove into the dooryard of Thomas's little house and boldly met the suspicious eye of his wife, who was peeling potatoes at the back door. She admitted that her husband might possibly be found if he were sought in the swamp down over the hill, where he had gone a couple of hours before to clear out the alder bushes; and thither I proceeded, making the last stage of my journey over treacherous hummocks which frequently turned out to be mere tufts of long grass, inviting the sole of the foot to descend and then blandly subsiding under its weight into the spongy surface of the swamp. By this uncertain and frequently disastrous mode of advance I finally reached the spot where the bushes were being laid low under the furious onslaughts of Thomas's double-bitted axe. I then secured a substantial hummock, grasped one of the surviving alder bushes for support, and introduced myself while Thomas regarded me with a stern and menacing eye.

The mention of my fine old-fashioned Scotch name brought a friendlier gleam into the fierce eyes that were steadily bent upon me, and the animosity finally vanished altogether before the discovery that we were on the same side of politics. The stirring campaign for reciprocity was at its height, and Thomas and I clung to our respective bushes for upwards of an hour while we threshed over the familiar arguments to be made by "the poor man" in favor of letting down the bars of protection. Thus, when the time came for me to attempt a transition to the unrelated topic of music, Thomas was quite ready to accompany me in a spirit of sympathy. He admitted at once that he had been accounted a fair singer in his day, whereat my heart leaped up; then he went on to boast that his voice, during its prime, had been the strongest one in the church choir, whereat my heart subsided. Religion may be strong to uplift and to save, but it is not one of the forces that aid in keeping the ballads alive in these troublous times.

My dark forebodings presently clarified themselves into a shape all too definite. Thomas followed up his boast by taking a firmer grip of his bush with one hand, while with the other he propped himself resolutely upon the support of his axe. Then he fixed a solemn eye upon me and broke into a wild minor strain which is familiar to every Scotchman who knows the psalmody of his fathers. The words fitted to this strain are variable, and in the version of Thomas they began thus:

> Broad is the road that leads to death,
>   And thousands walk together there;
> But wisdom shows a narrow path,
>   With here and there a traveller.

The volume of sound was terrific. I rocked and swayed on the frail foundation of my chosen hummock as the little church at the village must have rocked in the days when Thomas demonstrated his vocal superiority in its choir; and all the while I was under the necessity of giving my entertainer gaze for gaze. To have looked anywhere but into the steely orbs that were fixed upon me would have been to signify that the champion voice of the old kirk choir was at last failing to be impressive; therefore I looked and listened like a three years' child while Thomas thundered along towards the period of his lugubrious hymn.

After I had bestowed upon this performance the full meed of my hypocritical applause, I proceeded slowly but with a steady insistence to draw Thomas towards the realm of profane and popular music. Finally I became definite and specific and asked him pointblank if he had ever heard a song called "The Seven Brethren," illustrating my question by a direct quotation from a ripe old popular ballad that I had copied down from the lips of an ancient singer earlier in the summer:

Arise, arise, ye seven brethren,
  And put on your armour so bright—
Arise and take care of your youngest sister,
  For your eldest went away last night.

"Ah, yes," roared Thomas in a reminiscent tone, "I mind of me mother singin' that song when I was a boy. Let me see how it goes!" Then, taking a firmer hold of his alder bush, he sent his voice hurtling through the quiet air:

Arise, arise, ye seven brethereen
  And put on your armours bright—
Arise — — —

Beyond this point the song, of its own accord, would not transport the singer, and Thomas, though he put forth efforts both herculean and stentorian, could not budge it one word further. Finally he acknowledged himself a beaten man. "Me mother," he asserted mournfully, "used to sing that song and a hundred more like it; but she's been in her grave many a year, and I never bothered with the old songs after I went into the choir."

I felt even more dejected than old Thomas. He had only made a manful attempt to entertain me for an hour or so in the way which had seemed best to fit my desires, but I had falsely possessed myself, in anticipation, of a priceless store of ballads which now, in a moment, had slipped from my grasp forever. And, since Thomas had proved to be a broken reed and a stricken alder bush, it remained for me only to put the final question which I keep in stock for the conclusion of a fruitless interview: "Do you know of anybody around these parts that might be able to sing any of the old songs?"

"Why, yes," said Thomas, cudgelling his brain in a pathetic eagerness to make amends for his recent failure, "there's old Ann Thompson in yon little house up over the hill. They tell me that she used to have a lot o' them old songs that she would sing for the boys when they was dancin' and fiddlin' at her house. Ye might try her—if she'll let ye git past her dooryard."

It is the trade of the ballad-collector to walk up to roaring lions chained in caves and to attack fortified cities whose walls perchance will tumble at the blast of a trumpet; therefore I did not hesitate at the prospect of storming the little house, up over the hill, which immured the grim and mysterious figure of old Ann Thompson. As I hitched my horse to the post safely placed outside the debatable ground of the dooryard, I cautiously noted, upon a bench in front of the house, an ancient figure clad in an ancient gingham gown ending well above a pair of frankly displayed bare feet which were disposed for coolness upon the grass. The face was thin, angular, and cynical even in profile; and as for the eyes, they were not once turned in my direction as I noisily approached, but remained fixed upon the distant and inscrutable sea.

Too long and tedious were it to tell of the protracted conversation in which I introduced, one after another, a rich and varied list of topics upon which I was freely allowed to expend the treasure of my oratory while Ann made occasional brief and sarcastic responses. The chances are that I should presently have unhitched my horse with never a ballad upon the writing-pad in my inside pocket had not a stout ally come to my assistance in the person of a sonsy matron who approached around the corner of the house rubbing her hands free of the flour from her last baking of bread. The eyes of the newcomer were mild, as those of her father must have been, and when she introduced herself as the daughter of the dour, black-eyed dame upon the bench, she smiled at me in friendly and comfortable fashion. Before professing herself ready to serve me to the height of her ability she insisted only upon a complete and detailed account of my occupation and lineage, and these are topics on which I am always prepared to be cross-examined by the ballad-singer and the ballad-singer's family. When my catechism was completed I stated modestly that my ruling passion was to hear old songs and to copy them down on paper.

"Good land!" exclaimed my ally heartily, "that ain't very much to ask for. Mother has a lot o' them old songs if she'll only sing them for ye." Then she made a direct appeal to the unresponsive figure upon the bench,— "Mother, why can't ye sing a few o' yer old songs for the man? It won't hurt you and it won't hurt him."

Ann had been listening intently without appearing to do so, and without once shifting her gaze from the distant Strait of Northumberland; but now she rolled her black eyes for an instant upon her daughter, and then more deliberately upon the face to which I was struggling to impart an expression of preternatural honesty. "Yes," she said, "I'll sing me songs for him, an' a great time he'll have, when he goes back to the village, tellin' them about the fun he had with old Ann, settin' around on her bare feet singin' foolish old songs."

Many lovers, since the world began, have to their mistresses given vows of eternal fidelity, swearing by the bright moon, the stars of heaven, and the sands of the desert; but no lover did ever protest as I protested to Ann that day. She was forced to relent—or, rather, to seem to relent, for she now began to dissemble in crafty fashion. "Ah, well," she said, "I did use to sing once, when I was younger an' spryer than I am now, but I could no more sing for ye now than I could fly. . . . Emma," she went on, turning to her daughter, "go an' fetch that book of old songs from the house. He can write some o' them down, an' they're a blame sight better than any I could give him."

The daughter labored off hopefully to find the book, quite satisfied, in her innocence, that old Ann had hit upon the device for ending all our difficulties. As for me, I bided my time as does the captain of a storm-beaten bark when morning dawns and he sees the distant headland which shelters the haven for which he sails. The ballads were here, and I assured myself inwardly that I would be hung up by the heels in the market-place but I would write some of them down before I crossed Ann Thompson's dooryard again. When the book was in due season placed in my hands I dissembled in my turn as craftily as Ann had done, examining with great care the words and music of "Old Black Joe," "Swanee River," and many other lachrymose ditties which failed to draw the responsive tear from my iron lids.

"There are plenty of songs better than these," I remarked after a space, "and they've never been written in books either. Take a song like this one, now," and, lifting up my voice, I huskily carolled the first two stanzas of a brave old "Come all ye" ballad of Waterloo:

Come all you brisk and lively lads,
    Come listen unto me,
While I relate how I have fought
    Through the wars of Germany.

29

I have fought through Spain and Portugal,
  Through France and Flanders too,
But it's little I thought I'd be reserved
  For the plains of Waterloo.

"Ho!" exclaimed Ann sardonically, "so ye know that one, do ye? Well, there's plenty more like ye that knows it too, but I have a song about Waterloo that I'll bet ye never heard from anyone but me!" And, imbued suddenly with the enthusiasm of the old singing days, she broke into a tuneful utterance of the unique ballad:

As I walkèd out on a fine summer's evening—

Here the song abruptly halted, and my heart came to my throat with the fear that Ann's enthusiasm had died in the moment of its rebirth. But she calmly announced, "That next line's gone. Perhaps, if you're a great scholar, ye can make one up to put in." Then, without giving me a chance either to succeed or to fail in this scholarly test, she proceeded with the song:

There I heard a damsel make a sad lamentation
  About her absent lover on the plains of Waterloo.

"And ere that he left me he gave me a token,
  A gold diamond ring that was broken in two:
'You have my heart and ring, dear lovely Sally,
  To remember your dear Willy when he's far at
    Waterloo.'"

I said, "My pretty fair maid, ye pride of all nations,
  Can I but be so bold as to ask your true love's
    name?
For I have been in battles where cannons loudly
  rattle,

30

And by your description I might have known
   the same."

"O, William Smith's his name, he's a hero of fame."
   "Many's the battle him and I have been in.
Through Portugal and Russia we often marched
      together.
   He was my loyal comrade through France and
      through Spain.

"As by the French we were all surrounded,
   Like bold British heroes we did them subdue.
We fought three days together until we did
      subdue them,
   Like bold Napoleon Boney on the plains of
      Waterloo.

"By French soldiers your true love was slain

          .   .   .   .   .

It's there I saw him lie, there I saw him bleed
      and die
   With his low faltering voice he bid me adieu."

Here a whole stanza was gone, as Ann freely admitted,
piecing up the imperfection with an explanatory comment: "She would fall down in a faintin' fit, not knowin'
that it was her own true lover she was talkin' to in the
dark." Then the triumphant conclusion was presented by
the song itself:

When he found her so loyal he pulled out the token,
   The gold diamond ring that was broken in two,
Saying, "You have my heart and ring, dear lovely
      Sally,
   To remember your dear Willy, but he's far
      from Waterloo."

Mangled and battered and torn though it was, this ballad had firmly implanted itself in the affections of old Ann, and its very wounds rendered it doubly dear, for they remained as a proof of what Ann repeatedly boasted, that no one else could sing the song differently because no one else knew it. As for me, I welcomed it as gladly as "dear lovely Sally" welcomed her lòver who so cruelly tested her faith in the treacherous gloom of a summer evening.

If a ballad-singer can be persuaded to give you one song he will then proceed to hand over to you every song that he possesses, regretting only that he has not more to give; also, it must be remembered that old Ann and I had exchanged ballads in the process of singing to each other, and this is a ceremony as formal, binding, and sacred as the halving of a "gold diamond ring." A few minutes after the singing had ended we all proceeded, an amicable trio, towards the single entrance to the cottage, while Ann made one last hypocritical attempt to put me in my place. "I s'pose," she remarked to her daughter, "I'd better put on me boots an' me silk stockin's before I go to set up in the parlor with him."

I have narrated, in rather aimless fashion, this double adventure of my ballad-hunting days, not because the adventure is of any special interest in itself, but because it truly illustrates the discouragement, failure, and chance success that form the mingled lot of the ballad-collector in these latter days. Ballad-gathering is no longer an "attempt of ease," but the collector who knows that it will soon be quite impossible will not refuse to accept his share of discouragement if now and then he is enabled to record a traditional song that after-ages will not willingly let die.

CHAPTER THREE

My First Ballad-Hunt

In the following two or three chapters I shall give a rambling account of my first adventures in pursuit of the ballad, and I may quite properly preface the account with a brief sketch of my preparation for the work. This sketch may be narrowed down to the simple statement that I have always been addicted to what is frequently described as "low company." Since I was reared in a Nova Scotia seaport town, where the grades of society go down as low as heart could desire, I had for years ample opportunity of satisfying this base-born predilection to the full; and when I developed, a few years ago, the nobler ambition to form a collection of the Nova Scotia ballads I had the best stock-in-trade obtainable for the purpose, a familiarity with the sort of people who now possess a monopoly of this very humble species of entertainment. Still, I would not have anybody think that my youthful experience made the task of collecting ballads a simple one. No possible kind of preparation for the work could effect that result, and if it were necessary for me to choose a text for my remarks my text would be, The way of ballad-collectors is hard.

My first introduction to ballad-singing as a matter of oral tradition was through an old man of French descent known as Little Ned, though, as he himself never forgot, he had for special use on dignified occasions the sounding name of Edward Langille. Little Ned was a cobbler in the village of River John, and in his diminutive hut, imminent upon the river bank, he plied his trade and entertained at all hours those of his acquaintances whom he saw fit to advance to terms of intimacy. He lived as completely in the past as if the clock had ceased to move, many years before, when he had reached the prime of life; and in consideration of his garrulity and his marvellous memory—a natural enough accompaniment of complete and hereditary illiteracy—he was a most delectable companion for one who could appreciate a vivid reproduction of "the old days."

Little Ned was thus a most happy exception to the rule which I presented so mournfully in my first chapter. He had no sort of objection to enlivening the present with the entertainments of the past, for the simple reason that the past was still the present to him. Of the new and fashionable tendency to sing tearful ditties about gay ball-rooms and deserted homes he never knew, or, knowing, was serenely oblivious. Moreover, like many an one whose usual rôle it is to play the part of bland entertainer, Little Ned was at all times guarded against contradiction or ridicule by the suggestion of a strong potential irascibility; and in his own castle, which he rarely forsook, his point of view was constantly maintained.

Among his various spoils of the past Ned had a stock of ballads which, in age and variety, was probably without parallel in the whole countryside. When in a tuneful frame of mind—a condition easily produced in his case by the gentle influence of a little rational stimulant—he would sing ballads by the hour with never a regret for the half-finished piece of cobbling on the bench beside him. Among the older ballads in his collection his favorites were, "Lord

34

Thomas and Fair Ellinor," "Little Matha Grove," and, above all, "Bolender Martin." But the songs in his repertory were not all drawn from the lists of older English and Scottish popular ballads. He was equally interested in the misfortunes of the Prince Edward Islander who introduced the story of his life by informing his hearers:

"O my name is Peter Ambelay, as you shall understand.
My home is in Prince Edward Island, down by the
    ocean strand."

Frequently he discharged the duty of instructing his youthful visitors through the medium of a moral ballad depicting an unhappy person who began life by "steering his course for pleasure" and who came to grief in the sequel. Or, if the occasion was more merry, he would sometimes troll out a ditty beginning,

O there were three Boston ladies,
    And they were dressed in green,

which, by contrast with most of his songs, had the airy effect of a bit of *vers de société*.

I must be pardoned for dwelling at some length on the memory of this antique purveyor of the old ballad stock. Even now, after the lapse of several years, I cannot reflect upon the rich possibilities of Little Ned without much inward pain. After leaving home for college I saw very little of him for some years, but when I became interested in the ballads as literary documents, and had my eyes opened to the importance of gathering traditional versions now extant, my mind naturally reverted to the ample

35

store-house of old Ned, which I could open for the asking. I determined to spend a part of my next summer vacation in ransacking the store-house for the benefit of mankind, but no sooner had I formed this honorable resolution than I received a letter from home stating that my old friend had suddenly died.

Ballad-singing has for many years, and in the richest fields, been on the point of lapsing from a moribund state into positive extinction. The north shore of Nova Scotia, as I have come to believe, is a very rich field as fields go nowadays, but it is irredeemably impoverished by the loss of such a singer as old Ned Langille. Practically all of the ballads in my collection I have procured from men and women in the neighborhood of seventy or eighty years of age. With that generation the singing of ballads as a recognized form of entertainment seems to have ceased, and any persons of a younger generation who have acquired ballads traditionally have done so because of some unusual condition of character or circumstance, and not because it was a conventional or desirable thing to do. Therefore, the sort of persons that one may speak of now as forming the chief class of ballad-singers are men and women who have survived to the age of eighty or thereabouts, who were ballad-singers in their young days when ballad-singing was more fashionable, and who have in some way managed to retain portions of the old ballad stock through the years that have elapsed since it passed out of fashion. In the light of these facts I claim the right to bestow the passing tribute of a sigh upon the memory of Ned Langille the cobbler.

But ballad-singing, though it had been dealt a heavy stroke by the death of Little Ned, had not yet utterly perished from the earth, and in the summer of 1909 I started out in rather aimless fashion to wander through the country in search of people who were old, who were musically inclined, and whose social status did not elevate them above the plane of vulgar amusements. First of all, I decided to pay a visit to old Susan, a surviving sister of Little Ned's, in the wavering hope that she might be a chance possessor of some of the material which had, all too late, caused her brother to assume such important dimensions in my sight. She lived in the hamlet of Marshville, about five miles from her brother's earthly residence, and thither I directed my steps one broiling July afternoon.

Reaching her home, I was admitted to the combination sitting-room, dining-room, and kitchen where she and her husband were sheltering themselves from the sun, and partaking, instead, of the more personal and private species of heat emitted by the roaring wood-fire in their kitchen stove. The husband was further adding to the domesticity of the scene with a comforting pipe of Pictou twist, the most concentrated narcotic in existence; so, in order not to infringe on the harmony of the scene, I put my own pipe into operation before entering upon a discussion of the weather and the briefness of human existence. A consideration of the various ills that torment the mortal flesh naturally enough included a passing mention of the recent death of Ned; and here I succeeded in introducing my own topic, in spite of old James's absorbed interest in his own condition and his deepening conviction that he was a dyin' man, that's what he was, a dyin' man.

Susan was inclined to sniff at my assertion of her brother's superiority in the realm of song. "Ah," she sighed, "Ned must a' told ye that. He's dead and gone now, pore

Ned, but there's no denyin' that he used to be a terrible liar." I stoutly maintained that, liar or no liar, Ned had entertained me time and time again with songs in great variety and profusion. "O yes," she admitted, "Ned knowed a few songs, but he could never sing like his father. *He* was a singer for ye, now, was me father. When I was a girl I can mind of him settin' on his bench and tap tappin' on the shoes, an' singin' songs that would bring the very tears to your eyes. He could sing steady all day an' never sing the same song twict." A modest request for a reproduction of some of these tender ballads drew from Susan only a repeated insistence on their great variety and their potency in forcing tears to the eyes. "I never hed any music in me head," she explained, "it all run to me heels."

I become conscious that I am doing an injustice to the personality of this kindly old lady. She had become convinced that I was in a state of desperate physical ill-being, and she was much more concerned about some remedies for my lean and depleted appearance than about the pedantries of ballad-lore. But the short of the matter is that she could not sing or repeat a single line of the multifarious ballads that her father had sung. The best she could do was to give the substance of two that had especially appealed to her "because they was so sad"—"Lord Thomas and Fair Ellinor" and "James Harris, or the Demon Lover." Apart from these she had only a general impression that a great many of her father's songs had been about "fightin' and love, an' lords an' ladies."

But, with a real desire to do everything that could be done for my entertainment, she finally suggested that her own man used to know a couple of songs; whereat old

James, seeing the attention directed his way, spat judicially into the blazing inferno of the kitchen stove and admitted that he might be able to produce one song if he was
allowed to "study fer a while."   After a short period of
"studying" and another ineffective bombarding of the fire
he closed his eyes, leaned back in his chair, and proceeded
to rasp out in a very hoarse voice a ballad which I should
like to present in full,—partly because, as I learned sub-
sequently, it once enjoyed a wide popularity in the community, and partly because it has in my eyes a large ex-
trinsic interest as being the first ballad that I set to paper:

O come all ye men of learning, and rambling boys beware.
It's when you go a hunting take your dog, your gun, your
    snare.
Think on lofty hills and mountains that are at your com-
    mand,
And think of the tedious journey going to Van Dieman's
    Land.

O there was three men from Galloway town, Brown, Mar-
    tin, and Paul Jones.
They were three royal comrades, to their country they
    were known.
One night they were trapanded by the keeper of the strand,
And for seven long years transported unto Van Dieman's
    Land.

O Brown he had a sweetheart, Jean Summer was her
    name,
And she was sent to Dublin town for the playing of her
    game.

Our captain fell in love with her and married her out of
    hand,
And the best of treatment she gave us going to Van Die-
    man's Land.

O the place we had to land upon was on some foreign
    shore.
The people gathered around us, about five hundred score.
They yoked us up like horses and sold us out of hand.
They chained us to a chain, boys, to plough Van Dieman's
    Land.

O the place we had to sleep upon was built of sods and clay,
And rotten straw for to lay upon, and dare not a word to
    say.
The people gathered all round us, saying, "Slumber if you
    can,
And think of the Turks and tigers that's in Van Dieman's
    Land."

O one night as I lay upon my bed I dreamed a pleasant
    dream.
I dreamed that I was in old Ireland down by a spurling
    stream,
With a handsome girl upon my side, and she at my com-
    mand—
When I woke quite broken-hearted all in Van Dieman's
    Land.

A modest enough beginning to my labors, in good sooth.
Of the many ballads and songs that I have collected from
time to time this is one of the humblest and the least. And
yet it did not fail to win its tribute of emotion from poor
old Susan, who in the judging of a ballad must be allowed

to have had some qualifications which are denied to those of greater erudition. As the singing proceeded she evinced the liveliest sympathy for the luckless "Brown, Martin and Paul Jones," and kept ejaculating sorrowfully: "Oh, the pore fellahs!" "To think they had nawthing but rotten straw to lay on!" and so forth. And her husband, far from being annoyed by this running fire of most audible comment, sang with greater vigor and was visibly heartened by the realization that he was arousing emotion by his performance.

This is one of the few occasions on which I have witnessed the satisfactory—I might almost say the ideal—rendition of a ballad, and my memory of the composite performance of old James and his wife is to me rather more valuable than is the somewhat debased and sentimentalized ballad which I carried away. It is only when a ballad is rendered by a singer of the old school in the presence of one or more listeners who have by chance survived with him that the full significance of ballad-singing can be realized. The total effect is infinitely greater than that suggested by the unanimated ballad which is transmitted to the printed page, or even by the words with the music. It is both of these plus the emotion of singer and listeners, an emotion manifested by the latter, sometimes in ejaculatory comments, and sometimes in an unconscious or excited joining of forces with the singer in the rendition of a line or a refrain. In this harmony between the singer and his audience one may see, if one is as fortunate as I have been, a clear suggestion of that older and more complete harmony which the dust of many centuries has so obscured for us, and which we vaguely define as "the spirit of the throng."

41

CHAPTER FOUR

THE DISCOVERY OF BOB

A week or two after my rather uneventful afternoon in the torrid clime of Susan's kitchen I heard by a sort of accident of an old man who seemed specially designed by a sympathetic Providence to serve my peculiar ends. One of the friends to whom I told the story of my quest was a doctor in Tatamagouche, a village about twelve miles from River John; and among his patients was an octogenarian named Bob Langille, who lived a couple of miles outside of the village with his two sisters, and they, also, were well stricken in years. Bob was unable to repay the doctor's services with coin of the realm, but on one or two occasions he had shown his gratitude to his benefactor by singing some old songs which he evidently regarded with a lover's jealousy and with a father's pride. So ran the report of the doctor, who agreed to convoy and to introduce me in proper form, since, as he very sagely observed, I should be in danger of expending much eloquence to little purpose if I should go unsponsored. Accordingly, thus stoutly attended, I set out one morning for the humble abode of the ancient trio.

We found our potential ballad-singer in the little dooryard behind the house, making feeble efforts to split a block of wood. He greeted my friend with the profoundest respect, acknowledged my introduction to him, and immediately disappeared within the house. We followed him as far as the kitchen to pay our respects to the two

42

old sisters, who were enjoying the unseasonable comforts of a blazing wood fire. After I had given a fairly complete account of my parentage, occupation, and place of abode in answer to the insistent demands of the sisters, Bob reappeared, having in the meantime exchanged his tattered "cow's breakfast" for the more ceremonial headgear of an antique felt hat. This he continued to wear, except for the brief intermission of dinner-time, during the rest of the day, in honor of his visit from two professional gentlemen.

This action on the part of old Bob immediately suggested a comparison between him and my departed friend, Little Ned. The latter had always received his company with the dignity of a king on his throne extending greetings to an embassy, and had worn his fur cap summer and winter, indoors and out, with never a misgiving as to the fitness of his attire. But this is subjecting poor old Bob to a severe and rather unfair test. In an age of victorious and overpowering conventionality it is too much to expect that one should encounter another unconscious and serene individualist like Little Ned.

But while these reflections were flowing with the undercurrent of my mind I was laboring with great vigor to ingratiate myself with the ancient trio, who were subjecting me to a careful scrutiny. At length Bob loudly avowed that he would be the willing servant of any friend of the doctor's, the latter went on his way, and Bob and I retired to an inner room, an apartment almost bare of ornament or furniture, but happily separated by a partition from the torrid clime of the kitchen. Here we began to review the situation.

"It's seldom I sing me songs to anybody nowadays,"

said old Bob. "The time was when a man was thought somethin' of if he could set up fer a whole evenin' and sing the old English songs, but now a man's no good onless he kin sing these new-fangled Yankee songs with no sense nor no story to them."

It soon appeared that, as this prologue suggested, Bob was a Britisher of intense and blazing patriotism. "Onct I sung a song fer a Yankee sailor about the Chesapeake and the Shannon," he announced. "It was a good song too, an' it told about the British beatin' the Yankees like they deserved." "He was a younger man than I was," he added gleefully, "an' he'd a' licked me fer it if they hadn't been too many Britishers around fer him."

It may seem strange that this flaming enthusiasm for the British flag should exist in a man who, as his name indicates, was of French origin, but the fact is that the same uncompromising loyalty towards an adopted rather than a parent land is manifested by all the people of Bob's age, race, and condition of life in that particular part of Canada. Much of our conversation that morning was about the Battle of Waterloo, and Bob became as excited over the topic as if he had just received news of the downfall of Napoleon. Bob's elation was of a general and British character, but Little Ned, who was never tired of discoursing on the same great theme, had always shown particular zeal over the prowess of "de Scotch Greys." Without their able assistance, he had argued, Wellington could never have won the victory.

In a later chapter I shall give reasons for the apparent recreancy on the part of the French people who settled in Nova Scotia. The fact, which is enough to state now, is that they immediately went to work to take over the tra-

Old Bob had been in his day a mighty singer of ballads.

ditions—folk-lore, patriotism, and all—of the Scotch settlers with whom they were associated and from whom they
learned the English language. Old Bob, Little Ned, and
their fathers before them, received from their exiled ancestors of two or three generations back something of the
French temperament, appearance, and manner of speech,
but in the way of tradition and belief they had nothing
which had not been borrowed from their neighbors in the
adopted land.

By these repeated excursions from my entertainer to
topics merely suggested by my recollections of him I may
give the impression that I was then subjecting my new
acquaintance to the cool scrutiny of the man of science.
Nothing could be further from the truth. My whole endeavor was to establish myself in the character of sympathetic and interested auditor, and in this I was so far successful that I could at length feel that there would be no
offense in suggesting that a good old-fashioned song should
be produced to enliven the occasion. Bob leaned forward,
fixed his gaze earnestly upon a knot in the floor, and
"studied" for a few moments; then, throwing back his
head and closing his eyes, he began with a suddenness and
a volume of sound that for the moment harrowed me with
fear and wonder. It would not have seemed possible,
without auricular evidence, that such a frail old body could
be made the propelling power for such thunder-blasts of
music. The voice was now cracked and hoarse, and peril-
ously uncertain on the upper notes, but the evidence was
clear on the point that old Bob had been in his day a
mighty singer of ballads.

His manner of delivery was different from that of Little Ned and of many other singers whom I have heard

more recently. They, as a rule, sang with a careful re-tardation on the last words of each stanza; but Bob pro-ceeded from line to line, and from stanza to stanza, with the greatest rapidity and vehemence. On the last line of the song, however, he practiced the device which has been used by every ballad-singer that I have ever listened to, that is, he sang the first part of the line in the regular way with eyes closed and head thrown back, then made a swift and sudden descent from the empyrean of music, opened his eyes, leaned forward, glared upon his audience, and pronounced the last few words in an emphatic conversa-tional tone.

This, as it seems to me, is a most effective way of ap-prising the audience that the story is rounded out and brought to a victorious conclusion. It is—to introduce an easy and unstrained analogy—as if Pegasus had completed his flight, brought his rider safe to ground, and allowed him to spring lightly from his seat to converse with earth-treading mortals before beginning the next ascension. And the symbolic action employed for the production of this effect is frequently reënforced by an emphatic impact of the right hand upon the knee.

The first song had no title that Bob had ever heard. "Ye kin call it what ye like," he assured me when he saw my anxiety to know how it had been referred to in the days when it was a song worth knowing. One would not have to seek far for the implied title, but since from Bob's point of view the song was of great importance and the title negligible, I shall out of respect for his memory give the song in full:

THE DISCOVERY OF BOB

'Twas of a beautiful damsel, as I have heard it told,
Her father died and left her five thousand pounds in gold.
She livèd with her uncle, as you may plainly see,
And she loved a ploughboy on the banks of sweet Dundee.

Her uncle had a ploughboy. Young Mary loved him well,
And in her uncle's garden her tales of love would tell.

. . . . . .

. . . . . .

One morning very early, just at the break of day,
Her uncle came to Mary, and then to her did say,
"Arise, young lovely Mary, and come along with me,
For the young squire's waiting for you on the banks of
    sweet Dundee."

"A fig for all your squires, your dukes and lords besides,
For young William he appears to me like diamonds in my
    eyes."
"Hold on," said her uncle, "for revenged on you I'll be,
For I will banish William from the banks of sweet
    Dundee."

The press-gang came on William as he was all alone.
He boldly fought for liberty though there was ten to one.
The blood did flow in torrents, he fought so manfully.
He'd rather die for Mary on the banks of sweet Dndee.

One morning as young Mary was lamenting for her love,
She met the wealthy young squire down by her uncle's
    grove.
He put his arms around her. "Stand off, base man,"
    said she,

. . . . . .

He put his arms around her and strove to throw her down.
Two pistols and a sword she spied beneath his morning
gown.
Young Mary took the pistols, the sword she handled free.
She fired and shot the squire on the banks of sweet
Dundee.

Her uncle overheard the noise and hastened to the ground.
"Now since you've killed the squire I'll give you your
death-wound."
"Keep off," then says young Mary. "Undaunted I shall
be."
She fired and shot her uncle on the banks of sweet Dundee.

A doctor he was sent for, a man of noted skill.
Likewise there came a lawyer for him to sign his will.
He signed all his gold to Mary, who fought so manfully.
He closed his eyes no more to rise on the banks of sweet
Dundee.

Young William he was sent for and speedily did return.
As soon as he arrived upon the shore young Mary ceased
to mourn.
The banns were quickly published, their hands were joined
so free.
She now enjoys her ploughboy on the banks of sweet
Dundee.

The wall of reserve was now demolished, and behind the
ruins appeared a fair garden of cantatory fervor, from
which Bob continued, without any urging from me, to send
forth resounding peals of music. Indeed, my chief trouble
now was to persuade him to pause occasionally and give
me a song in such form that I could copy it out. He sang

so rapidly that no human being without the accomplishment of shorthand could possibly follow his voice with pen and paper. Then, when he attempted to repeat the song without the music he had to go pretty rapidly in order to maintain the continuity of his recitation; and ever and anon he would forget a line and suddenly burst into a loud roar of song, which meant that he was "backing up" to go through the whole stanza in the hope of catching the stubborn line off its guard.

But the chief of my troubles on this morning arose from a different cause. I may explain that I was still the veriest amateur at the great sport of stalking the ballad, and had not yet learned the various marks by which the more experienced hunter distinguishes his prey. The "English and Scottish popular ballads" of Child's collection I had become familiar with; and, with Little Ned's "Lord Thomas and Fair Ellinor" and "Bolender Martin" haunting my memory, I had set out solely to procure variant versions of the true old stock. Everything else was dross in my sight, and, while I copied out as many of old Bob's songs as I could, I did so, as I thought, merely to gratify my own private curiosity.

But to return to the performance of Bob, in which, I think it may safely be assumed, the reader is more interested than in the discomforts of Bob's audience. There were other ballads of the same general nature as the one I have cited,—brave tales of distressed but resourceful maidens and young men of humble birth and noble qualifications; and, interspersed among these, were some stirring tales of sea-fights with pirates or with the national foes of Britain. These sea-ballads were held in the greatest esteem by Bob, and the particular one that found su-

preme favor in his eyes was "The Little Fighting Chance."
The reasons for this will be readily found if I present the
ballad itself:

On the fourteenth of July once so clear was the sky.
We saw a sassy frigate come bearing down so nigh,
Come bearing down upon us as we sailed out of France.
The name that she was called was The Little Fighting
    Chance.

Chorus.
    So cheer up, my lively boys. Let it never be said
    That the sons of old Britannia would ever be afraid.

If I had been a listener of the good old-fashioned sort I
could not have sat gazing silently and impassively at
the singer who was making this passionate appeal to my
loyalty and manliness. This lack of the proper response
in me put upon old Bob the constraint of piecing up my
imperfections in himself, and, as he delivered the last word
of the brave chorus, he opened his eyes, glared upon me
with an access of patriotic fervor, and bellowed, "They
never was afraid yit, me boy!" Then, having supplied the
comment which he should have had merely to stimulate,
he closed his eyes and proceeded with redoubled vigor:

We gave to them a gun and the battle had begun.
The cannon they did roar and the bullets they did fly.
It was broadside for broadside. We showed them gallant
    sport.
And to see the lofty yards and the topmasts rolling over-
    board.

The Discovery of Bob

We fought them four hours, the battle was so hot,
Till four of our foremost men lay dead upon the spot.
Sixteen were wounded, made twenty in all.
And down with the French lily, boys, the Frenchmen one
and all.

O now, my brave boys, since the prize is our own,
What shall we do for jury-masts? for spars we have none.
So we tore in with a sweet and pleasant gale,
And early the next morning to the feet of our king sail.

O now, brave boys, since we have gotten safe to shore,
We'll make the ale-houses and the taverns for to roar.
Here's a health unto King George and all his gallant fleet!
We'll smother all the Yankee dogs that ever we do meet.

The reader of the uninspired line might easily dismiss "The Little Fighting Chance" as an incoherent, half-rhymed, metreless attempt at poetic narrative. But I, who have heard it delivered with conviction by one who was in his own way a severe enough critic, cannot regard it so lightly; for I cannot forget how lovely and pleasant to Bob was the imagined relegation of French lilies, Yankee dogs, and all things offending the good King George, to one indiscriminate slaughter-bed.

The song which followed this is brief enough to present in full. Its interest lies in the fact that it shows a very neat combination of the two apparently irreconcilable topics which have been taken up separately in the two ballads just presented,—the dauntless maid and the English victory at sea.

As we were a sailing down by the Spanish shore
Our druns they did beat and the guns loudly roar.
We spied a lofty admiral ship come ploughing down the
 main,
Which caused us to hist our tops'ls again.

Come, boys, let us be hearty, come, boys, let us be true,
And after our enemy we quickly shall pursue.
Soon as we overtake them upon the ocean wide
With foresail set we'll give them a broadside.

They gave to us another as good as we sent.
For to sink each other was our whole intent.
At the very second broadside our captain he was slain.
Up steps a damsel his place for to maintain.

"O quarters, O quarters, my brave British boys."
"No quarters, no quarters," the damsel she replies.
"You have the best of quarters I can to you afford.
You must fight, strike, or sink, my boys, or jump over-
 board."

Now since we gained the victory we'll drink a glass of wine.
Drink to your own true love and I'll drink to mine.
Here's a health unto the damsel, the damsel of fame,
So boldly she fought on the Union by name.

As Bob sang I made efforts to copy, or, when the motion was too swift for me, I leaned back, closed my eyes
in imitation of my entertainer, and resigned myself to the
pleasant task of learning some of the tunes. The two old
sisters hovered about, as Othello says of Desdemona,

But still the house affairs would call them thence,
Which ever as they could with haste dispatch
They'd come again and with a greedy ear
Devour up Bob's discourse.

If the song happened to have a refrain they would join
in, and frequently they would accompany him through a
line or a stanza which had lodged itself in their memories.
And at all times they commented freely on the stirring
events which their brother was celebrating in stentorian
song.

Finally it reached the hour of high noon, and as I had
no desire to forfeit the esteem of the two sisters, who were
becoming more and more impressed by my friendly and
conciliatory manners, I cast false delicacy to the winds and
accepted their invitation to join the family at their meal
of boiled potatoes, mammoth slices of bread, and tea that
had been boiled until a spoon would stand upright in it.
Bob laid aside his hat and drew up to the board, but in
him the spirit of poetry was not wholly supplanted by
gross desires for bread. "Ther was a man once," he announced, as he laid his folded hands upon his plate, "that
made up a piece of poetry for a blessin' on his dinner, and
I'll give it to ye:

Some hev meat and cannot eat,
And some would eat that hev no meat,
But we hev meat and we kin eat,
And so God bless the giver.

"Amen!" responded old Maggie fervently; and, ceasing to reflect upon the cavalier treatment that verse re-

ceives during the process of oral transmission, I addressed myself to the business in hand.

While we were partaking of the food thus consecrated, Bob and his sisters were moved to discourse upon that period of their lives which had been called up by the performance of the morning. Though they were now living hard by the sea-coast, they had spent their earlier years in New Annan, a Scotch settlement about twenty miles inland. Bob had been a cobbler by trade. He had worked his bit of land in season, and, when occasion called, had gone from house to house building and repairing shoes. His love of ballads was such an early growth that he could not remember the time when he had not immediately appropriated and tucked away in his capacious memory every new one that came in his path; and since in his capacity of itinerant cobbler he had visited from time to time most of the homes in a singing community, he had had ample opportunity of acquiring new songs in exchange for old ones. "Ah, sir," cried old Kitty, moved by these reminiscences to a burst of enthusiasm for the splendor of the past, "it was nawthin' but singin' an' dancin' in them days. Many's the time we would take hold of hands an' go through the fields to a dance singin' the old songs together."

After the family had moved down to Tatamagouche, which was about thirty years before I made their acquaintance, Bob had learned most of his sea-songs, and these, I suspect, had had the effect of crowding out some of the older ballads which he had learned in New Annan. They had, of course, made their special appeal to his fervid patriotism, which would give them an advantage over most of the "English and Scottish popular ballads" of the older days; but, even so, if my suspicion is just, it presents a distant limitation to Bob's title to be considered as a prophet of conservatism. Little Ned, and his father before him, had been brought up also in one of these inland Scotch districts, very near New Annan; and they, as I found out by inquiries from time to time, had sung their old traditional Scotch ballads to the end, with very few additions of newer material. Little Ned was in every way a more conservative person than Bob, though the latter was far from being a slave of fashion, and clung tenaciously to what he considered old in music as in other things. The difference, then, is merely one of degree: Ned's conceptions of the old were more consistent and extreme than those of Bob.

We may now return to the dinner-table, where bread, potatoes, and tea were ceasing to play their part. When we finally pushed our chairs back and proceeded to load our pipes, Maggie, the younger of the two sisters, announced that she had a song that she was going to sing for me "while Bob was gittin' rested up." I cheerfully bade her sing on, and she at once composed herself and began with a plangent vigor which showed that she had studied her brother's methods to some purpose. Her song was the "Gaspard Tragedy":

In Gaspard of late a young damsel did dwell.
For wit and for beauty few did her excel.
A young man did court her for to be his dear,
And he by his trade was a ship-carpenter.

He said, "Dearest Mary, if you will agree,
And give your consent, dear, to marry me,
Your love it can cure me of sorrow and care,
Consent, then, to wed with a ship carpenter."

With blushes as charming as roses in June
She answered "Dear William, to wed I'm too young;
For young men are fickle, I see very plain.
If a maiden is kind her they quickly disdain."

"My charming sweet Mary, how can you say so?
Thy beauty is the heaven to which I would go.
And if there I find channel if I chance for to steer
I there will cast anchor and stay with my dear."

But yet 'twas in vain she strove to deny,
For he by his cunning soon made her comply,
And by base deceptions he did her betray.
In sin's hellish paths he led her astray.

Now when this young damsel with child she did **prove**
She soon sent her tidings to her faithless love,
Who swore by the heavens that he would prove true,
And said, "I will marry no damsel but you."

Things passed on a while. At length we do hear
His ship was a-sailing, for sea he must steer,
Which pained this poor damsel and wounded her heart,
To think with her true love she must part.

Cried she, "Dearest Will, ere you go to sea
Remember the vows you have made unto me.
If at home you don't tarry I never can rest.
O how can you leave me with sorrows oppressed?"

With tender expressions he to her did say,
"I'll marry my Mary ere I go to sea,
And if that to-morrow my love can ride down,
The ring I can buy our fond union to crown."

The Discovery of Bob

With tender embraces they parted that night
And promised to meet the next morning at light.
William said, "Mary, you must go with me
Before we are married our friends for to see."

He led her through groves and valleys so deep.
At length this poor damsel began for to weep,
Crying, "Willie, I fear you will lead me astray,
On purpose my innocent life to betray."

He said, "You've guessed right. All earth can't you save,
For the whole of last night I was digging your grave."
When poor Mary did hear him say so
The tears from her eyes like a fountain did flow.

"O pity my infant. O spare my poor life.
Let me live full of shame if I can't be your wife.
O take not my life lest my soul you betray,
And you to perdition be hurried away."

"There is no time disputing to stand,"
But instantly taking a knife in his hand
He pierced her fair breast, whence the blood it did flow,
And into the grave her fair body did throw.

He covered her body and quick hastened home,
Left nothing but the small birds her fate to moan.
On board ship he entered without more delay,
And set sail for Plymouth to plough the salt sea.

A young man named Stewart of courage so bold
One night happened late for to go in the hold,
Where a beautiful damsel to him did appear,
And she in her arms held an infant most dear.

Being merry with liquor he went to embrace,
Transported with joy at beholding her face;
When to his amazement she vanished away,
Which he told to the captain without more delay.

The captain soon summoned his jovial ship's crew,
And said, "My brave fellows, I'm afraid some of you
Have murdered some damsel ere you came away,
Whose injurèd ghost now haunts on the sea.

"Whoever you be, if the truth you deny,
When found out you'll be hanged on the gallows so high,
But he who confesses his life we'll not take,
But leave him upon the first island we make."

Then William immediately fell to his knees.
The blood in his veins quick with horror did freeze.
He cried, "Cruel murderer, what have I done?
God help me, I fear my poor soul is undone.

"Poor injurèd ghost, your full pardon I crave,
For soon I must follow you down to the grave."
No one else but this poor wretch beheld the sad sight,
And raving distracted he died that same night.

Now when her sad parents these tidings did hear,
Soon searched for the body of their daughter so dear,
In the town of Southampton in a valley so deep.
Her body was found, which caused many to weep.

In Gaspard's green churchyard her ashes now lie,
And we hope that her soul is with God in the sky.
So let this sad tale be a warning to all
Who dare an innocent young maid to enthrall.

This time it was Bob's turn to act the part of bystander and to evince a sympathetic interest in the progress of events. He became more and more wrought up as the heroine's fortunes darkened, and his excitement grew overpowering as the singer described poor Mary's grief when the perfidious William prepared to execute his master-stroke of villainy:

He led her through groves and valleys so deep.
At length this poor damsel began for to weep,
Crying, "Willie, I fear you will lead me astray,
On purpose my innocent life to betray."

Then followed the cool and murderous response of William:

He said, "You've guessed right. All earth can't you save,
For the whole of last night I was digging your grave."

This was too much for human endurance. "The damn scoundrel!" roared Bob, "I wisht I hed him be the throat fer a minute or two!" Then, with a renewed sense of the pathos of the situation, "Ah, the pore gyurl! I can't keep the tears out o' me eyes when I think of her!" But his sister, swelling with importance over the applause she was evoking, had now got several lines beyond the point that had stimulated Bob's wrathful outburst.

I have written the song down as it fell from the lips of Maggie, but I have been enabled to do so because she sang it for me on a subsequent occasion after my wife and I had hit upon the scheme of copying songs line about in order to double the speed of the work. If I had to rely upon the results of this my first visit, the "Gaspard Tragedy" should go unrecorded so far as I am concerned. It impressed me then as being one of the most interesting songs I had heard that day, and I at once made the effort to copy it; but I might as well have tried to capture a wireless message. Old Maggie could make an easy and unhesitating passage through the ballad on the wings of song, but, divested of these wings, she became incapable of the slightest progress; nor could she, though with the best intentions, go slowly enough with her singing for me to get the words down.

But at this unhappy juncture Bob, who had been earnestly "studying" with his head in his hands, suddenly leaned back with his eyes tightly closed, and resolved himself into a tornado of song:

> Arise, arise, ye seven brethren,
>   And put on your armours bright.
> Arise and take care of your younger sister,
>   For your eldest went away last night.

Then was the oil of gladness straightway poured upon my troubled head, for this was an "English and Scottish popular ballad" at last. Old Kitty and I settled our backs against the wall and drew on our pipes with a contentment which no elusive ship-carpenter could mar, while Bob, raging like one inspired, whirled onward through the reverberating stanzas.

> 'Twas on the road, 'twas away they rode,
>   'Twas all by the light of the moon,
> Until he looked over his left shoulder
>   And saw her seven brethren drawing nigh.

"Lie down, lie down, Lady Margret," he said,
  "And by my two steeds stand,
Until I fight thy seven brethren,
  And thy father, who's nigh at hand."

She stood and saw her seven brethren fall
  Without shedding a tear,
Until she saw her father fall
  Whom she lovèd so dear,

"Withhold thy hand, Lord William," she said,
  "For thy stroke it is wonderful sore.
For it's many's the true love I might have had,
  But a father I'll never have more."

She took her white pocket-handkerchief,
  That was made of the hollands fine,
And wiped her father's bloody bloody wound
  That run redder than the wine.

"Choose ye, choose ye, Lady Margret," he said,
  "Will you here abide?"
"O no, I must go wheresoever you go,
  For you've left me here no guide."

He mounted her on his milky white steed,
  And he on his dappled gray.
The bugle horn hung by his side,
  And slowly they rode away.

'Twas on the road, 'twas away they rode,
  'Twas all by the light of the moon,
Until they came to the Erint waters,
  That was raging like the main.

He lighted down to take a drink
  Of the spring that run so clear,
And down the stream run his good heart's blood.
  Sore she begun to fear.

"Lie down, lie down, Lord William," she said,
  "For you are a slain man."
"O no, it is your scarlet red cloak
  That's reflecting on the main."

'Twas on the road, 'twas away they rode,
  'Twas all by the light of the moon,
Until they came to his mother's chamber door,
  And there they lighted down.

"Arise, arise, dear mother," he says,
  "Arise and let us in,
For by all the powers that is above
  This night my love I've won."

"O mother, mother, make us a bed,
  And sheathe it with the hollands fine,
And lay Lady Margret by my side
  And sound sound sleep we'll take."

Lord William he died at the middle of the night,
  Lady Margret ere it was day,
And every true lovers that goes together
  I wish them more luck than they.

When Bob opened his eyes upon the last line of the ballad I was waiting with raised pencil to conduct him through a second and more prosaic recital; and when I left the abode of song late that afternoon, with my right arm hanging limp from the shoulder, my comfort was that I had, at least, discovered one gleaming nugget in the mine of base metals.

CHAPTER FIVE

Rimes of an Ancient Mariner

The sophisticated reader—that is to say, the reader who is sophisticated in folk-lore—will have perceived that the preceding chapter is an account of the early struggles of an extremely innocent and amateurish collector. As a matter of fact, when I made the rich discovery of old Bob and his songs I was merely a young person with a recently acquired college diploma and with a chance enthusiasm for the English and Scottish popular ballads. My imagination had been fired by a reading of Professor Child's great collection, and I had noted with a growing excitement that many of the best numbers in this collection were reminiscent of the songs with which, in my salad days, I had been entertained by Little Ned Langille. I began my intermittent search, then, only with the desire to preserve some local versions of the genuine old stock. But the rather more enlightened view of the situation which I obtained during the next winter presented Bob in an entirely new light. I learned what every ballad collector must learn if he is to continue his work without discouragement, namely, that no popular version of any sort of ballad, ancient or modern, can be regarded as common or unclean; and on the strength of this realization I determined to give my endeavors a somewhat wider range during the next summer.

One of the most interesting and picturesque figures in my natal village of River John was an old sailor named

Dick Hinds. During his youth and prime Dick followed the sea intermittently; then he settled down for good and all in the village. Here he wrought as occasion offered or as chill penury demanded, and here as elsewhere he fashioned many a subtle demonstration of his great discovery that the world is flat. Times without number, in my youthful days, I have looked on while Dick, with pencil or chalk in hand, has sketched his plan of the world on a plank, a wall, or whatever medium was for the moment available; and have heard his triumphant challenge to the onlookers to prove that our so-called sphere was not as flat as the background on which it was then being represented, or to maintain, if they dared, that any spot on this uncurving expanse could reasonably be called North Pole or South Pole.

Dick had various devices for holding off the gaunt wolf, and one of these was to serve at times as night watchman in the old saw-mill on the river-bank. Thither, on winter evenings, would I repair joyously, to be received with the same cordiality and good-fellowship as if I had been the old sailor's equal in years and in understanding. He would make up a couple of rough couches in a warm spot behind the boiler, and there I would recline at ease and listen to such wisdom as no schoolbook ever afforded. London and Liverpool were glowingly described from the sailor's point of view, the political situation in Canada was critically reviewed, and the Scriptures were freely expounded. But whatever the topic might chance to be, it was always introduced by a leading question, propounded with great apparent severity, though Dick's only purpose was to bring the topic clearly and strongly before his hearer, and he never asked the question without having his own answer ready to give after a suitable pause for further emphasis. "What," he would ask, for instance, "What did the Lord mean when he said, 'I will establish the throne of my sarvent David?'" A brief silence would ensue, while Dick gazed into fathomless space and emitted huge clouds of tobacco-smoke. Then the pipe would be removed, the eyes sharpened and trained on the listener, and the answer delivered with startling vigor and conviction,—"What but the throne of England, and no other place on airth? England, the ruler of the world, the rock of science, and the seat of larnin'!"

Among Dick's fascinations for the young was an inexhaustible and richly varied stock of songs far exceeding in interest any that I ever heard at school. There were accounts of the daring robberies and the last heroic fight of "bold Jack Donahue," of the matching of wits between sailor Johnny and his Liverpool landlady, and of the terrific battle at sea which terminated the career of Kelly the Pirate. With these and with countless others was my youthful heart moved more than with a trumpet.

When I began my search for ballads I knew perfectly well that Dick's complete stock, such as it was, could be made mine for the asking. But as I was aware that he had no songs with the flavor of great antiquity to recommend them, I did not consider at first that they were worth the asking. However, when the second summer came round, and I arrived upon the scene with my eyes opened to the true state of affairs, I lost no time in making up for my previous neglect.

In my discussion of Bob Langille I spoke of the sea-songs as having rather marred the harmony of his earlier repertory; but Bob's collection was homogeneity itself compared with Dick's. The latter had begun by learning some traditional ballads current in Nova Scotia in his youth; during his seagoing days he had acquired further ballads and countless sea-songs from his companions in the forecastle; and he had added to the complexity of the list by making several additions gathered from the streets, wharves, and music-halls of the various cities which he had visited in his travels. This puzzling collection he himself regarded with great calmness and impartiality, and there were only two specimens that he marked for special approval. These were "Kelly the Pirate" and "Jack Donahue." The first I shall have occasion to discuss in another chapter, but the second I should like to present here. In one form or another it has been sung in Australia, Great Britain, Canada, and the United States; and this is one of my reasons for presenting Dick's version, which is more detailed and complete than the ones usually found. But my chief reason is that I have heard Dick sing it so often and so ardently that without it my recollections of him would be strikingly incomplete.

Come all you gallant bushrangers and outlaws of disdain,
Who scorn to dwell in slavery or wear the brands of chains.
Attention pay to what I say, and value it if you do,
I will relate the matchless fate of bold Jack Donahue.

This bold undaunted highwayman, as you shall understand,
He was banished for his natural life from Erin's happy land.
In Dublin city of renown his first breath ever he drew,
And his deeds of valor entitled him of bold Jack Donahue.

He scarcely then had reached his fate on the Australian
    shore
When he took to the highway as he had done before.
There was Matha Mar, and Jack Woods, and Warbly and
    Wangelo too,
They were the four associates of bold Jack Donahue.

He happened to be taken in the middle of his prime
And banished for the natural life for that outrageous
    crime.
But he left all the constables of Sydney in a stew,
And before they reached the Sydney jail they lost Jack
    Donahue.

He scarcely had made his escape till a-robbing he went
    straightway.
The people were frightened to travel the roads by night
    and day.
And every day the newspapers would publish something
    new
Concerning of that highwayman they called Jack Dona-
    hue.

As Donahue and his companions walked out one afternoon,
Little thinking of the brands of death that would afflict
    them soon,
To their surprise the horse-police well armèd came in view,
And in quick time they did advance to take bold Donahue.

Said Donahue to his companions, "If you'll stand true to
    me,
This day I'll fight for liberty, and that right manfully.
To be hanged upon a gallows I never intend to do.
This day I'll fight until I die," cried bold Jack Donahue.

"O no," said cowardly Wangelo, "such things can never be.
Don't you see there's eight or ten of them? It's time for
us to flee.
And if we wait we'll be too late, and the battle we'll surely
rue."
"Then begone from me, you cowardly dogs," cried bold
Jack Donahue.

The sergeant said to Donahue, "Discharge your carabine.
Or do you intend to fight with us or unto us to resign?"
"To surrender to such cowardly dogs I never intend to do.
This day I'll fight for liberty," cried bold Jack Donahue.

"Now if they had been true to me I would recall their
fame.
But now the people will look on them with scorn and great
disdain.
I'd rather range the wild woods round like a wolf or a
kangaroo
Than I'd work one hour for government," cried bold Jack
Donahue.

The sergeant and the corporal they did their men divide.
Some men fired behind him and others at his side.
The sergeant and the corporal they both fired at him too,
Till at length a ball it pierced the heart of bold Jack
Donahue.

Nine rounds he fired and shot five police before the fatal
ball
That pierced the heart of Donahue and caused him for to
fall.
And as he closed his struggling eyes he bade the world
adieu.
Kind Christians all, pray for the soul of bold Jack
Donahue.

"Woman! the companion of man an' he's rock of salvation in times of affliction an' sorrah."

There is in this ballad a fine resonance and a rhetorical sweep that made a large appeal to Dick, whose own speech savored richly of these qualities. But even in such cases as this, where his enthusiasm was greatest, his manifestation of it was of the briefest duration. Opening his eyes as he delivered the last line, he would smite his knee vigorously and in a loud voice announce the name of the song: "Jack Donahue the Highwayman!" or "Kelly the Pirate!" and then lapse into that meditative mood which was the prelude to some high theme such as the House of Lords, "the only body of free men in the Parlyaments of the world." Or, if the ballad happened to be a tale of the dauntless maid who has always been so dear to the popular imagination, some such question as this would follow: "What is the noblest creature that God ever created on airth?" Then in due time would come Dick's own ringing response: "Woman! the companion of man an' he's rock of salvation in times of affliction an' sorrah!"

When Dick was minded to uphold such hypotheses as this last one he had small support from the quarter where he should most have expected it. His wife, whom he treated with distinguished courtesy, calling her "Lady Hinds" in moments of expansion, always met these rhapsodies with disdain, and would interrupt her husband's flight with a request to "stop his fullish talk an' go on with his singin'." Whereat Dick would stoutly maintain that he meant what he said and that no one knew this better than Lady Hinds herself. But in the end he always made a practical demonstration of his sincerity by giving in goodnaturedly and proceeding with the next song.

In the brief space that I have allotted to Dick in these chronicles it would be utterly impossible for me to give

any just conception of the infinite variety exhibited by the
songs and ballads which he sang for me from time to time.
I visited him repeatedly in order to procure the fresh ones
that kept rising to the surface of his memory, and, although on many successive occasions he gave every outward sign of being "sung out," he would just as regularly
meet me a day or two later with the hearty greeting, "I
thought up another song fer ye last night after I went to
bed. Bring yer missis around any time an' ye can have
it." Besides, when ladies and gentlemen are spending a
social evening together they can hardly be expected to put
in all their time at the mechanical business of repeating
and copying songs.

Many of Dick's ballads had evidently made their first
appeal to him because they presented tales of picturesque
heroes with sounding names. I have already suggested
this in the case of Jack Donahue. Other protagonists
were Dick Turpin, Jack Shepard, and the great soldier of
Canadian history who, in Dick's glowing version, is thus
pictured in the hour of his crowning triumph:

> Brave Wolfe drew up his men
> In a line so pritty
> On the plains of Abraham
> Before the city.

But countless other heroes in the collection were nameless,
or appeared under such nondescript appellations as John
or Frank. Of the latter sort was the chief actor in "The
Liverpool Landlady," a ballad which was given to me in
one form by Dick, and in another, under the title "Green
Beds," by Bob Langille. Dick's version begins with the
terse expository stanza,

I'll tell you a story, I'll not keep you long,
Concerning a sailor whose name it was John.
He made a gallant voyage to sea and just returned to
    shore.
He was ragged and dirty as though he was poor.

The last line hints vaguely, but truly, that John may
not be quite so poor as he seems, and this fact is discovered
with tragic belatedness by his Liverpool landlady, who
at first refuses to give him credit or to allow him to court
her daughter, and then makes a gross and ineffectual attempt to treat the whole affair as a joke when John thrusts
his hands into his ragged pockets and brings them out
loaded with gold.

This ballad, standing as it does with "one foot in sea
and one on shore," must have awakened tender memories
in many a listener in the fo'c'stle. Dick had several examples of such amphibious song, notably "The Tiger and
the Lion." This one, however, barely touched the solid
earth before plunging out to sea and into a series of adventures culminating in a ship-to-ship encounter in which
"bold Dighton" led his followers to a glorious and complete slaughter of the French. But I had much better
allow the ballad to appear and demonstrate in its own
proper person its adventurous character and sounding
quality.

Come all you bold seamen that ploughs the rough main,
Give ear to my story, the truth I'll explain.
There was a misfortune in sad time of war,
And how we escaped from the French at Bastar.

There were seamen bold, three hundred and more,
Was shut up in prison on Guadeloupe shore.
They were chained down in prison and sorely oppressed,
By painful diseases and famine oppressed.

There was a bold seaman, from St. Lords he came,
He was generous in action, called Dighton by name.
He had the heart of a lion, the soul of a prince,
Through honour and friendship to us did advance.

He came to the prison to bemoan our sad fate,
He launched out his gold to relieve our sad state.
Five hundred guineas he paid down, and more,
Which much did relieve us in that distressed hour.

At this generous action the French did complain.
It was then they bound him in fetters and chains.
They threw him in prison with us, you may see.
From his fetters and chains, boys, he soon set us free.

"Come all you bold seamen, if you take my advice,
Stand true to my side, it is done in a trice.
Down in yon portway the Tiger she lays,
She's a well-found staunch cruiser, she's fit for the sea.

"The captain's on shore and all things on board.
There's plenty of cannon, pikes, pistols, and swords.
And if you prove valiant and stand by my side,
Never fear but we'll board her and sail the next tide."

At this generous action we all did agree
To break out of prison to die or be free.
Two gallant young sailors as his seconds he chose,
And a signal of freedom was, "Death to the foes!"

Then out of the French prison we all rushed amain.
Two big guns was fired, the French guard was slain.
And down to the Tiger we all took our way,
We slipped both her cables, and steered out for sea.

Their forts being opened, right on us did play.
The shot flew like hail as we got under way.
They battered our spars as we sailed from the shore,
To bid them a good-night a broadside did pour.

Then early next morning we thought ourselves clear.
But for our mistake, boys, we paid very dear.
'Twas early next morning just as day we spied
The Lion of Pervert bearing down alongside.

She supplied us with broadsides, which grieved our hearts
 sore,
Which caused the bold Tiger to make her guns roar.
With twenty-six eighteens the Lion did howl;
With eighteen brass fours the Tiger did growl.

'Twas yard-arm and broadside together did lay
Till a shot from the Tiger took his mizzen away.
Now said bold Dighton, "If you're tired of the fun
You have got your choice, to fight or to run."

To shun blood and slaughter we all did incline.
To run from the Lion it was our design.
But to our misfortune and our sad distress
That very same moment they grappled us fast.

They tried for to board us thrice over in view,
But they were opposed by the Tiger's bold crew.
They trebled our metal with men three to one,
But Fortune still favoured old Britain's bold sons.

Then up speaks bold Dighton, like a hero did feel.
His eyes glanced like fury, like the bright varnished steel.
"Come each of you seamen on the point of your sword.
It's death, boys, or freedom. We'll all jump on board."

Then over the bulwarks we crushed on our foe.
One clip from his sword laid the French captain low.
Then down on the decks, boys, their weapons let fall,
And on us brave heroes for mercy did call.

Swords rattled, pikes, pistols, the swords loud did clash.
The blood on our decks like water did splash.
The huge streams of crimson from our scuppers did pour,
And the blue sea around us ran purple with gore.

"It's now," says bold Dighton, "since the battle is o'er,
Let the French learn a lesson, go teach it on shore;
Let them go home to their country, and tell them beware
For to treat well in future the prisoners of war."

We cleared our decks that very same day,
The wind from the sou'west, we got under way,
And down to Antigua away then we bore,
And early next morning we all went on shore.

Here's a health to bold Dighton, a true valiant friend.
May honour protect him, and glory attend.
And when he is dead I pray you'll draw near,
And kneel at his tombstone and let fall a tear.

When Dick had concluded his sonorous rendition of
this ballad I was moved to ask him the idle question, "How
do you suppose this song came to be written? Did some-
one who was in the battle make up a song about it after-
wards?"

"Oh, good fortune!" cried Dick in amazement. "Them fellows could never write poetry like that! It would be Lord Byron or Tom Moore, or some o' them great poets of England."

In Dick's topography of human endeavor, it will be seen, all roads lead to England, and in his more recent conversations with me his theory was extended with absolute consistency to the tragic situation in which England has lately been playing her part. Even when the fortunes of the Allies were at their lowest ebb Dick would inquire with that conviction of tone which made his questions more conclusive than another man's assertions, "Do ye think they can ever conquer England, the home of liberty, an' the land which is now prosecutin' the glorious work of God?" Then, after receiving from me the inevitable response, he would bring his clenched fist upon his knee with the brave challenge, "Never shall it be said that a foreign army has set its foot upon the soil of England!" Nor did he fail to evolve an explanation of the fact that the great war was being fought out upon French soil. "France," he asserted one evening, "is a great country but a wicked one. She has sinned against the Lord in times past, and for that reason the war will be fought and decided within her gates. Ye'll find it all in the Bible. The judge that sentenced our Saviour to he's death was Pontius Pilate, wasn't it?" I assented to this apparently unrelated premise. "Well," resumed Dick, "after Pilate had finished the business an' signed the docaments sentencin' our Lord to the cross he went to bed, an' Missis Pilate was layin' there beside him, an' she went to sleep an' had a great vision of what was to come to pass in the future. She seen that our Saviour was an innocent man, an' that in time to come her an' Pilate would be banished to Gaul, an' that the great war of the nations would be fought where her and her wicked husband was to end their lives. An' so it has come to pass. The country of Gaul is now the country of France, an' the great war for righteousness and truth is now bein' fought on that ground where the murderer of our Lord ended he's days."

Many a problem raised by the great clash of the nations was worked out for me in similar fashion by Dick. It was very hard, indeed, for him to discourse on any other topic after the summer of 1914. But from his consciousness there never faded the kindly realization that I had a greedy ear for old songs, and on the very evening when he propounded his great theory of Pilate and the war he brought himself up presently with the assurance that he had been thinking over some fresh songs for me to copy down. "I ben turnin' over some o' the old shanties in me mind the last day or two," he announced. "Here's a mains'l shanty that I used to sing for the men when we was gittin' squared away for sea":

One evening as I rambled down by the Clarence dock,
   Heave away, my Johnnies, heave away
I overheard an Irish girl conversing with Tap Scott.
   And away, my Johnny boys, we're all away to sea

She says, "Now Mr. Tap Scott, come tell me if you
   please,"
   Heave away, my Johnnies, heave away
"And have you got a ship of fame to carry me over the
   sea?"
   And away, my Johnny boys, we're all away to sea

76

"O yes, I got a ship of fame, a ship that does well sail,"
Heave away, my Johnnies, heave away
"She's lying in the Waterloo dock and taking in the mail."
And away, my Johnny boys, we're all away to sea

"We got all things now ready, tomorrow she will sail,"
Heave away, my Johnnies, heave away
"We've got five hundred passengers and two hundred bags
of mail."
And away, my Johnny boys, we're all away to sea

For fourteen days we sailed the seas, the wind it proved
right true,
Heave away, my Johnnies, heave away
With twenty-seven sailor boys our passengers well knew.
And away, my Johnny boys, we're all away to sea

The captain being an Irishman, as you can understand,
Heave away, my Johnnies, heave away
He launched out his little boat on the banks of Newfound-
land.
And away, my Johnny boys, we're all away to sea

O then the wind began to blow, it blew from the nor'west,
Heave away, my Johnnies, heave away
And then the seas began to swell, and we could get no rest.
And away, my Johnny boys, we're all away to sea

Bad luck to the Joseph Walker, she rolled us head and
tail,
Heave away, my Johnnies, heave away
And the sailors they broke open the chests and stole our
yellow mail,
And away, my Johnny boys, we're all away to sea

Well, then we arrived in New York town, the place I
    thought so sweet.
    Heave away, my Johnnies, heave away
The very first place I found myself was down on Water
    Street.
    And away, my Johnny boys, we're all away to sea

Now I'm in Jack Montgomery's, I'll cock my yellow tail,
    Heave away, my Johnnies, heave away
So farewell, Mr. Tap Scott, likewise your yellow mail,
    And away, my Johnny boys, we're all away to sea

In addition to the shanties, of which he had a considerable number, Dick had gathered during his years before the mast a large and miscellaneous collection of sea-songs. Some of these were in ballad form, as, for instance, "The Old Ramillies," a harrowing tale of how the stout old ship "from her anchor cut and run" during a fearful storm, and how she finally went down, leaving only four to tell "How she behavèd in the gale." Still others were songs without any narrative, complaints of the hardships at sea mingled with praises of the brave, open, roving life of the sailor. One of these, which in the absence of a title Dick suggested should be called "Jolly Tars," runs thus:

    Come all you jovial sailors bold,
        The truth to you I write
    Consarning of the raging sea
        Which is my heart's delight.
    While the landsmen are on shore
        Little danger do they know,
    While we poor jolly sailors bold
        Must plough the ocean through.

They're always with their pretty girls
   A-telling them fine tales,
Telling them of the hard day's work
   They done in their corn fields.
It's cutting down the grass and weeds
   It's all that they can do,
While we poor jolly sailors bold
   Must plough the ocean through.

Soon as the sun it does go down,
   They'll throw away their hoes,
Saying, "We can work no longer."
   And homewards they will go.
As soon as ever it gets dark,
   It's into bed they'll crawl,
While we poor jolly sailors bold
   Must stand the bitter squall.

The night it is as dark as pitch,
   And the wind begins to blow,
The captain comes on the deck.
   Turn out, boys, from below.
All hands, all hands, on deck, my boys,
   And pay your ship regard,
And lay aloft, me lively lads,
   Send down the gallant yards.

We'll sail into all parts of the world
   That ever yet was known,
And we'll bring home all prizes
   From where we do return.
We'll spend our money freely,
   And go to sea for more,
We'll make the town to flourish
   When we return to shore.

In this group, also, might be included "Frank Fidd," a song of the "Tom Bowling" type, in which the employment of an abstruse nautical phraseology denotes a fine disregard of the landsman's limitations:

> Frank Fidd was as gallant a tar
>   As ever took reef in a sail,
> And when her lee gun'l lay under
>   He laughed at the noise of the gale.
>
> His grog he provide against storm,
>   While spitting the juice from his quid.
> Aloft, on the yard, or on deck,
>   It was all the same to Frank Fidd.
>
> One night off the Cape of Good Hope,
>   Head winds, our ship lyin' to,
> The bight of a rope catched Frank's heels,
>   And his head bulged on top of the flue.
>
> The doctor he sounded his brain
>   While the blood from his scuppers run fast.
> While soundin' Frank cried, "It's in vain,
>   For death it has broached me at last.
>
> "I'm afraid I'll away while I speak,
>   Life's capstan's hove taut on my heart.
> My anchor is now short apeak.
>   Don't you think I have acted my part?
>
> "I never feared danger or toil
>   Whilst a spark of life's blood was on deck.
> But now the last end of my coil
>   Is hove through eternity's block.

An intermittent sailor and man-of-all-work and a boisterous singer of a late variety of sea-songs.

"So, shipmates, no longer delay,
    Since life's but a span at the best.
And since I can cheer you no longer
    I'll mount o'er the truck of the blest.

"Safe moored in Felicity Bay,
    · I'll ride by the Cape of Delight.
What more can they say of poor Frank?
He's gone up aloft in a flight."

Though Dick was the most important personage with whom I labored in the ballad-field during the second summer of my collectorship, he was by no means the only one. From time to time I interviewed many people whom I suspected of having concealed ballads about their persons, and in some cases I was able to cajole them into admitting that they could "start one or two songs." But as I have pretty consistently given the impression up to this point that my labors were merely a round of social amenities, I must now, in support of the text which I proposed in an earlier chapter, present some evidence to show that the way of ballad collectors is hard. For this purpose I may employ the simple expedient of narrating my second visit to old Bob Langille.

During my first visit, it will be remembered, a state of idyllic peace and harmony had been established between the Langille family and their visitor. When I had made my farewells the two old sisters had patted my arm and assured me that I was just like one of themselves, while Bob, sending up clouds of smoke from the tobacco which we had shared like brothers, had stoutly and defiantly affirmed that I was a gentleman and a man among men. But now mark what happened a year later when I conveyed my wife to the Langille home to procure some of the ballads which it had been impossible for me to copy down on my former visit.

My wife remained outside in the carriage while I went round to the rear of the house in the expectation of finding Bob and reanimating the friendship of the previous year. I found Bob, but at that point my program was interrupted.

He was sitting on a log, with shoulders bowed, gaze directed earthward, and a total attitude of uncompromising dejection, while with his big clasp-knife he whittled slices from the side of a half-ripe apple and conveyed them to his mouth, from time to time, in a manner denoting a bitter lack of harmony with the world. He did not look up when I greeted him, and, as it was quite evident that he did not recognize my voice, I sat down on the ground, propped my back against the log, and proceeded to whittle a piece of wood in default of a half-ripe apple. The first part of the interview was mostly monologue on my part, but finally Bob was moved to state that the crops were bad, the weather damnable, and he himself on the high road to the graveyard.

"I suppose you don't remember me," I hinted respectfully at last.

"No," said Bob in a tone of discontented conviction.

"You sang some songs for me last summer," I suggested, in the vain hope that this might be the link that would fasten us in the bonds of amity again.

He peered over at me suspiciously with his dim old eyes. "I don't sing no songs," he asserted, with more vehemence than he had hitherto displayed. "It's time for me to be thinkin' o' me Bible, an' not about singin' songs."

I dropped the subject and accompanied him again to the more congenial topics of natural perversity, bodily illness, and the graveyard.

During a lull in the sombre dialogue I essayed to whistle a bar or two from one of the songs which Bob had refused to admit that he had sung for me a year before. Then I began boldly to sing the song, but had not proceeded far when I had to pause for lack of the right words. This was more than Bob could endure. With a sudden roar he took up the song at the point where I had faltered, and carried it through to a victorious conclusion. Then there was another song the tune of which I felt extremely uncertain about. Bob, now in a frenzy of zeal, set me right immediately. Then, as in former days, we filled our pipes from a common pouch, lighted them with a common match, and agreed on the superiority of all things that are ancient and British. In due time I led my horse into the back yard and introduced my wife; and Bob, loudly proclaiming that he would be our servant in all matters relating to song, led us indoors to the day's work.

Ballad-singers, without doubt, are uncertain, coy, and hard to please. The only complete exception to this rule that I have ever encountered was Dick Hinds the sailor, and he was an exception to all rules. It was not only his unvarying cordiality and his rich and florid eloquence that distinguished him from the throng of artisans who composed the conventional body of his peers. His unauthorized conclusion regarding the shape of the earth was merely one expression of the sturdy intellectual independence which imposed upon him, as it does upon all powerful individualities, a comparative loneliness in the midst of a complaisant society. His premises, to be sure, were not always complete or unimpeachable, but his conclusions were rigorous and consistent, and they were dignified by a passionate loyalty and an unfailing moral and physical courage. The foregoing chapter was written less than a year ago, and the present tense which I could then employ in my references to him I have since had to change to the past. In adding this concluding paragraph, therefore, I am composing a brief necrology for my brave old friend, but I should do much better to refer the reader to a set of verses which have taken on for me the significance of a memorial—the concluding verses of the song of Frank Fidd.

CHAPTER SIX

GENUINE ANTIQUES

It would be very easy and pleasant for me to ramble along with a chronological account of my adventures and of the various singers whom I have met from time to time, but I think that my subject will be better served if I proceed now towards something more in the nature of topical discussions. My work itself progressed in very intermittent fashion with the chronological order of the recurring summers, but I gradually became a more expert and seasoned fisher of ballads. Sometimes, like better men before me, I toiled all night and caught nothing; at other times there came to my net divers little fishes in the shape of murder ballads, ghost ballads, and other classifiable or nondescript specimens of small fry; and on rare occasions there would swim into my ken—if I may now twist my figure somewhat violently to meet the needs of my great argument—a new planet in the form of a genuine English or Scottish popular ballad. I shall now briefly discuss the specimens of the last-named sort which I have gathered in at one time or another.

As the shade of Julius Caesar broods over the action of Shakespeare's historical tragedy, so does the shade of Little Ned Langille brood over the activities of this humbler chronicle. It was my recollection of Little Ned's antique devices for entertaining his friends that first started me on the paths of collectorship, and there are few of my experiences upon these paths that do not in some way call up the memory of this stout old patron of the waning customs of an elder day. Year after year I have made it my special mission to track down the ballads which I remember by name or by description from his singing, and times have been when the guardian shade has presided over the close of a successful day, as will presently appear.

In an earlier chapter I explained that my first effort to fill the gap caused by Ned's death took the form of a visit to Ned's sister. Susan had admitted that "Ned might 'a' ben able to sing a few songs," and had further avowed that her father when in the prime of his powers could sing more songs than there were days in the year; but when I had inquired whether anyone was living in the neighborhood who might have inherited a few out of so vast a number she had defiantly asserted that there was not a single person then above ground who could sing one of them. In the light of facts more recently acquired I am now able to state that there was then living, within a mile of Susan's home, a younger brother of this same father who could sing all day without repeating himself. This brother, George Langille by name, was of course an almost incredibly old person, as may be judged by the fact that he was the uncle of Little Ned, who had not died until he was well stricken in years. George was, in fact, ninety-three years old at the time; but in his day he had also been a singer, and some prowess in song he retained to the end, concealing it jealously from everybody but his daughter, with whom he spent his last days.

These facts, however, were learned by me after George had been gathered to his fathers. The tragedy of it is that I did not learn them from his niece while he was

yet in the flesh. But to indulge oneself in murderous desires with poor Susan as the object would be entirely beside the point. She simply had not been taken into the
confidence of old George and his daughter, who in some
way had learned that in these degenerate days the ability
to sing old-fashioned songs was more likely to be regarded
with merriment than with envy, and who, like many others
who were once sweet singers in Israel, had found that it
better consorted with their dignity to hang their harps
upon the willows while in exile by the streams of Babylon.

When these mournful truths were brought home to me
they were accompanied by one suggestion of hope.
George's daughter, Easter Ann by name—or at least by
the popular rendition of her name—still remained above
ground. To her, accordingly, I prepared to resort; but,
since my mind was clouded with a doubt of my ability to
awaken candor in her breast, I proceeded, acting upon
an accession of undeniable wisdom, to enlist the services of
a doctor who had frequently repaired the body of old
George while it was still animated by the spirit. Accompanied by this important ally I proceeded with a stout
heart to the humble cottage of Easter Ann.

We were received with the respect due to gentlemen
with white collars on, especially as one of the collars en-
circled the neck of a doctor. After a fitting conversation
on the unusual prevalence of illness in the countryside and
the constant imminence of death, Easter Ann was asked
with much circumlocution and many assays of bias if her
father had not been a great singer in his day. She admitted that he had been, and further asserted that she saw
no great harm in singin' old songs if ye liked them, even
if everybody did look down on ye for doin' it. My friend

and I, however, had successfully driven home an impression of our catholicity of taste, for presently she informed me, in rather doubtful compensation for the loss of her father, "He wouldn't 'a' minded singin' for you and the doctor, though."

It was at length suggested that Easter Ann, having heard her father sing so often, might by chance remember a few of the songs herself. Well, she admitted cautiously, she might be able to mind of one o' them, but she had a very bad heart, and it would be a good deal better for all concerned if the doctor would examine that defective organ instead of settin' back and coaxin' her to sing foolish old songs. The doctor assured her that the rebellious heart would be looked into as soon as the song was finished, and finally she composed her elbows on the table, set her face resolutely to the front, closed her eyes, and began:

> 'Twas on a day, a high holiday,
>   The best day of the old year,
> When little Matha Grove he went to church
>   The holy word to hear,
>   The holy word to hear.
>
> Some came in in diamonds of gold,
>   And some came in in pearls,
> And among them all was little Matha Grove
>   The handsomest of them all,
>   The handsomest of them all.

This was the beginning of a rather mangled version of the superb old ballad "Little Musgrave," or "Little Matha Grove," as it had come to be during the process of oral transmission and oral transmutation. I shall come back to this ballad presently, but for the moment I must keep my attention courteously fixed upon Easter Ann.

When the performance was ended the heart was examined and found to be as sound as a dollar. In honor of this sudden restoration to health Easter Ann then proclaimed that she might be able to mind of a few verses from another old song. " 'Pretty Polly,' I sometimes calls it," she explained. We opposed no obstacle to this second performance, and she proceeded with an equally mangled but almost equally valuable version of the old ballad "Lady Isabel and the Elf Knight":

> There was a lord in Ambertown,
>   He courted a lady gay.
> And all that he wanted of this pretty maid
>   Was to take her life away.

"Did you say that 'Pretty Polly' was the name of the song?" I inquired when the last stanza was completed.

"No," asserted Easter Ann with sturdy finality, and with the evident suspicion that even I, with all my gentle ways, might be tempted to poke fun if I were given too obvious a chance.

"Well," I insisted, "wasn't it ever called by any name?"

"None that I ever heerd tell of," she answered, in a tone which implied that a profitless discussion had gone far enough, "but you've got plenty of larnin'. Make up a name for it to suit yourself."

This was Easter Ann's constant recipe for repairing broken or disjointed ballads. When she bungled a stanza or forgot a line her refuge always was, "But you can fix that up to suit yourself." This view of the question, I

may say, she held in common with the great majority of
the ballad-singers with whom I have toiled, and the curious thing is that not a single one of these people has ever
shown the least disposition to attempt the patching-up
process for himself. If a line were missing or a phrase
unintelligible that was none of their affair. They simply
sang the ballads—or supposed that they sang them—exactly as they had heard them delivered by some old and
authoritative singer, and they were willing to leave the
rest to me because of their confidence in my superior schol-
arship. I hasten to assure my readers that I have always
been at one with the singers in my respect for the authority of tradition, and have made no efforts to taint the in-
tegrity of the oral version as I have received it.

The two ballads which had so happily clung, battered
and bruised as they were, to the memory of Easter
Ann had been preserved in an interesting and rather curious way. Old George, as his daughter repeatedly assured
us, had been "a proud man," and this was one reason why
he had never chosen to sing his songs promiscuously or to
a potentially critical audience. But it is in matters of
personal appearance that Pride does chiefly operate, and
thereby hangs the tale. George when in the prime of life
had been adorned and beautified by a fine thatch of coal-
black hair, and as he proceeded through the years he regarded with increasing indignation the encroachment of
the inevitable white threads. At regular intervals, then,
he would summon his daughter to stand behind his chair
and pluck out these pallid intruders, while in payment for
the service he would sing these her two favorite old songs.
The white hairs reappeared and the songs were repeated
until, without any effort to acquire them for her own use,

the daughter had unconsciously come to the point where she could sing them herself.

I must now bid farewell to Easter Ann. But before doing so I should record a brief conversation which she held with me at a later date, and which, like all the conversations which I record, seems to me to have its value as a simple and illuminating commentary on the present status of the popular ballad. One day as I was driving past her house she came out with an admonitory hand upraised and implored me not to tell anybody that she had been singing crazy old songs for me. One of the neighbors, she stated, had approached the house on the day of my first visit, but, on hearing the barbaric strains within, had discreetly retired, reserving it for the following day to return and tell poor Easter Ann that she ought to be ashamed of herself. "I s'pose I oughtn't to sing songs like that," she concluded, "and me a member o' the church."

The two ballads given by Easter Ann were, as I have said, notably imperfect, and I immediately cast about for opportunities to revise them in the light of popular tradition. By means of a series of investigations which need not be explained here I finally unearthed (in the figurative sense) one Mrs. James Gammell, who was reported as having once been in the habit of singing "Little Matha Grove." Mrs. Gammell acknowledged, when pressed, that she had known the song years ago when she was a girl. After her marriage her husband, who had seen something of the world, had taken serious offense with her for singing "rowdy songs," and had finally induced her to renounce her degrading associations with the popular ballad. I stimulated her memory by repeating the version of "Little Matha Grove" which I had obtained from Easter Ann, and since her husband was dead and consequently in no position to impress the demands of respectability upon his wife, she was able to supply some few stanzas which had been omitted from the first version.

It is unnecessary to state that, warned by hard experiences, I now took the precaution of interviewing all those scions of the Langille family who might be laid under the least suspicion of familiarity with a popular ballad. Among these I found three who were able to make slight contributions to the increasing bulk of "Little Matha Grove." The final result was the composite version which I presented at the close of my first chapter.

I had an equal amount of success with the ballad which, since I have been given permission to call it what I please, I shall for the sake of convenience call "Pretty Polly." Among the relatives of Easter Ann with whom I reviewed the situation was a certain John Langille, an intermittent sailor and man-of-all-work and a boisterous singer of a late variety of sea-songs. John was not merely a relative of Easter Ann. He had the much larger distinction of being a nephew of Little Ned, in the light of whose countenance he had basked times without number. But with the blindness of a younger generation he had failed to perceive the rare qualities of his uncle's finest ballads, considering them as curious trifles rather than as songs worthy of being committed to memory for actual use. He could supply only a line or two of "Little Matha Grove"; but when we came to "Pretty Polly," he announced that he "used to roar this one a little" himself—"though," he added, he "never thought it was much of a song, either."

While the ballad-collector is pursuing his work he must on no account allow himself to attempt measures of reform,—in ballad singing or in anything else. His success will depend largely on his ability to regard every man's private opinions as his own sacred property. On the present occasion I made no attempt to convert John to the truth, but simply repeated Easter Ann's version to him and then allowed him to "roar it a little" himself, while I copied down several stanzas that were in much better condition than the ones I had already procured.

A composite version of this ballad I shall now present. The only additions which I made after my interview with John were variant versions of two stanzas, supplied by an old neighbor of Little Ned's named David Rogers, whom I discovered in a town about twenty miles away. David's recollections of the ballad were slim, as the paucity of his contribution will indicate, but he made up in part for this by an earnest assurance that whatever he supplied was sure to be right. In its finished form,* then, the ballad runs thus:

There was a lord in Ambertown,
   He courted a lady gay,
And all he wanted of this pretty maid
   Was to take her life away.

"Go get me some of your father's gold,
   And some of your mother's fee,
And two of the best nags out of the stable,
   Where there stands thirty and three."

She went and got some of her father's gold,
   And some of her mother's fee,
And two of the best nags out of the stable,
   Where there stood thirty and three.

---

* The ballad as I present it is, of course, the result of a combination of the best stanzas from the different incomplete versions that I found, and the variant stanzas I have simply had to omit.

She mounted on the milk-white steed,
   And he on the rambling gray,
And they rode till they came to the salt seaside,
   Three hours before it was day.

"Light off, light off, thy milk-white steed,
   And deliver it unto me,
For six pretty maids I have drownded here,
   And the seventh one thou shalt be.

"Take off, take off, thy silken dress,
   Likewise thy golden stays.
Methinks they are too rich and too gay
   To rot in the salt, salt sea."

"If I must take off my silken dress,
   Likewise my golden stays,
You must turn your back around to me,
   And face yon willow-tree."

He turned his back around about
   To face yon willow-tree.
She grasped him by the middle so tight,
   And she tumbled him in the sea.

"Lie there, lie there, you false-hearted man!
   Lie there instead of me!
For six pretty maids thou hast drownded here.
   Go keep them company."

So he rollèd high and he rollèd low,
   Till he rollèd to the sea-side.
"Stretch forth your hand, my pretty Polly,
   And I'll make you my bride."

"Lie there, lie there, you false-hearted man!
    Lie there instead of me!
For six pretty maids thou hast drownded here,
    But the seventh hath drownded thee."

She mounted on her milk-white steed,
    And she led her rambling gray,
And she rode forward to her father's door
    An hour before it was day.

The parrot being up so early in the morn,
    It unto Polly did say,
"I was afraid that some ruffian
    Had led you astray."

The old man on his pillow did lie,
    He unto the parrot did say,
"What ails you, what ails you, you pretty
    Poll parrot,
    You prattle so long before day?"

"The old cat was at my cage door,
    And I was afraid he was going to eat me,
And I was calling for pretty Polly
    To go drive the old cat away."

"Well turned, well turned, my pretty Poll
    parrot!
    Well turned, well turned!" said she.
"Your cage it shall be of the glittering gold,
    And the doors of ivory.

"No tales, no tales, my pretty Poll parrot,
    No tales you will tell on me.
Your cage it shall be of the glittering gold,
    And hung on yon willow-tree."

A few lines back I explained that, in my efforts to supplement the contributions made by Easter Ann, I interviewed all suspected members of the Langille family. Among these was a Mrs. Jake Langille, wife of a very friendly and mild-mannered farmer known as Devil Jake or Jake the Bear, in allusion to his ferocious appearance. Mrs. Jake was a grandniece of little Ned's father, and, furthermore, she had had the rare privilege of being reared in the presence of that great and inexhaustible fountain-head of ballads. The women-folks in this household had, as we may easily understand, been expected to adopt the rôle of listeners rather than of entertainers, in matters both of conversation and of song; but Mrs. Jake—or Lucy, as she was then—was inordinately fond of music, and she had contrived to pick up a few scraps of song as they were dropped by the lords of creation.

When the doctor and I made overtures to Lucy she became extremely nervous, and begged us piteously not to ask her to sing. She promised, however, to dictate a song to her daughter, who "was in the fifth grade at school and could write as well as the next one"; but we would have to give her a few days to get over the fright we had given her and to "study up" the song, which she had not thought of for years.

The promised ballad was duly received by me in the course of the week. In its manuscript form, however, it left much to be desired; consequently the doctor and I called upon Lucy once more, and by our friendly and ingratiating conversation wrought her up to such a pitch of boldness that she finally sang the ballad in our presence, just as though we had been mere women like herself.

It was "Lord Thomas and Fair Elinor," a very tolerable
version of the noble old ballad:

> Lord Thomas he was a worthy man,
>   He wore a sword by his side.
> Fair Ellinor was a beautiful bride.
>   Lord Thomas he loved her full well.
>
> "Come riddle, come riddle, dear Mother,"
>   he says,
>   "Come riddle us all in one,
> Whether I'll marry fair Ellinor
>   Or bring the brown girl at home."
>
> "The brown girl she's got house and land.
>   Fair Ellinor has got none.
> My son, if you will take my blessing,
>   O bring the brown girl at home."
>
> Lord Thomas he was a worthy man,
>   He wore a sword by his side.
> Fair Ellinor was a beautiful bride.
>   Lord Thomas he loved her full well.
>
> When he came to fair Ellinor's door
>   He knocked so loud at the ring.
> There was none so ready as fair Ellinor
>   To rise and let him in.
>
> "What news, what news, Lord Thomas?"
>   she said,
>   What news do you bring to me?"
> "I come to invite you to my wedding.
>   It is bad news for thee."

"The Lord forbid, Lord Thomas," she said,
  "If any such things should be.
I'm in hopes myself to be the bride,
  And you to be the bride's groom."

"Come riddle, come riddle, dear Mother,"
    she said,
  "Come riddle·us all in one,
Whether I'll go to Lord Thomas' wedding
  Or will I stay at home?"

"Many a one has been your friend,
  Many more has been your foes.
My girl, if you will take my blessing,
  To Lord Thomas' wedding don't go."
"Betray my life, betray my death,
  To Lord Thomas I'll go."

She dressed herself in riches so gay,
  Her merry maids all in blue,
And every gate that she passed by
  They took her to be some queen.*

When she came to Lord Thomas' door
  She knocked so loud at the ring.
There was none so ready as Lord Thomas
  To rise and let her in.

He took her by the lily-white hand
  And led her through the hall.
He set her on a golden chair
  Among the ladies all.

---

* It will be obvious to anybody acquainted with the old ballad, or with an
ear for rhyme, that the desirable word for the rhyme is "green" and not
"blue." I asked Lucy if she had never heard the word "green" here, which she
denied, but later, when I persuaded her to sing the ballad a second time she,
apparently unconsciously, substituted "green." However, since I had a hand in
bringing about the change I have not introduced it in the version that I present.

"Is this your bride, Lord Thomas?" she said,
　"I think she looks wonderful black.
You might have had as fair a one
　As ever the sun rose on."

"Despise her not, fair Ellinor," he said,
　"Despise her not to me.
For better do I like your little finger
　Than all her whole body."

The brown girl she being standing by
　With a pen-knife in her hand,
Betwixt the long rib and the short
　Pierced fair Ellinor to the heart.

"O what is the matter?"　Lord Thomas he
　　said,
　"I think you look wonderful pale.
You used to have as bright a color
　As ever the sun rose on."

"Are you blind, Lord Thomas?" she said,
　"Or can you not very well see?
Don't you see my own heart's blood
　Come dribbling down to my knees?"

Lord Thomas he was a worthy man,
　He wore a sword by his side.
He off with his own bride's head
　And dashed it against the wall.

He ordered a coffin to be made,
　A coffin both wide and long.
He ordered fair Ellinor at his right side
　And the brown girl at his feet.

This ballad, like many others which I am fortunate enough to remember, not as mere successions of lines and stanzas, but as vivid and resonant songs with appropriate music, moved to the Dorian mood of a sombre minor strain which even Lucy's timid and rather shrill delivery could not rob of its effectiveness. It will be noticed that the story comes to a somewhat abrupt and disjointed conclusion, and this was immediately remarked by Lucy herself, who paused before the last stanza and proclaimed in great distress that there was a verse in here that she couldn't remember to save her soul. After delivering the concluding stanza she went back and groped around desperately in the remote corners of her mind, but all that she could drag forth was the recollection that the missing stanza told about the death of Lord Thomas by his own hand.

In the shame occasioned by this lapse in conduct she was exceedingly anxious to make such atonement as lay within her power, and with this purpose in view she presently announced that she could remember part of an old song which her uncle used to sing for the women "when he was feelin' good-natured," and which was called "Barberry Ellen." I signified a willingness to listen, and she proceeded eagerly with the following version of "Barbara Allen," the most widely known and sung of all the surviving "English and Scottish popular ballads."

> It was the very month of May,
> And the green buds they were swelling.
> Young Jimmy Groves on his death-bed lay
> For the love of Barberry Ellen.

He sent his man down to the town
  In the place where she was dwelling.
"Make haste and come to my master's house
  If your name is Barberry Ellen."

Slowly, slowly she got up,
  And so slowly she came nigh him.
"I cannot keep you from your grave.
  Young man, I think you're dying."

He turned his back to her then.
  A deadly swound he fell in.
He bid adieu to all his friends
  And adieu to Barberry Ellen.

As she was walking in the plain
  She heard the death-bell tolling.
And every stroke it seemed to say,
  "O cruel Barberry Ellen."

As she was walking on the road
  She met the corpse a-coming.
"Lay down, lay down the corpse," she said,
  That I may look upon him."

The more she looked the more she laughed
  For the love that he had for her,
While all of her friends cried out, "For shame,
  O cruel Barberry Ellen."

When he was dead and laid in grave
  Her heart was struck with sorrow.
"O mother, mother, make me a bed
  For I will die tomorrow.

"Hard-hearted creature that I was,
  Who lovèd me so dearly.
O that I had more kinder been
  When he was alive and near me.

"Come young and old, both great and small,
  And shun the fall I fell in.
Henceforth take warning by the fall
  Of cruel Barberry Ellen."

Lucy was not the only member of her gifted family to whom I went weeping for the loss of Little Ned, and bearing the precious seed of my recollections of the old singer; nor was she the only one from whom I returned, at the close of the day, rejoicing and bearing my sheaves with me. As my quest proceeded I kept hearing occasional sinister references to one "Isaac's Ellen," who had left the community years before, but who, in her younger days at least, sang and danced and was "chuck full of the old boy." It appeared, moreover, that Isaac's Ellen had been attracted to profane music rather than to the psalms, hymns, and spiritual songs of the more civilized and godly among her neighbors.

From my selfish and biased point of view this description served only to make Isaac's Ellen seem lovely and desirable, and I diligently sought for her until I found her. She readily acknowledged that she had learned a good many ballads in former years, from the singing of her mother and her two uncles, who used to get together in the evenings and "sing old songs turn about." She was not at all sure, however, that any of these songs were of a nature to be acceptable to me. The fact is that Ellen had seen a bit of town life, and out of her experience she was suspicious that I might be a gentleman, and therefore above such entertainment as she could offer. I exerted myself vigorously, therefore, to convince her that in some respects I was no gentleman at all, and in this I succeeded so well that she finally proceeded to sing, though even then she selected her songs very carefully and kept a keen weather eye upon me for signs of annoyance or disdain.

Ellen had a very fair list of ballads which, on cautious consideration, she felt that she could venture to present to the person of delicacy and refinement that she still suspected me to be, but among these there were no genuine old "English and Scottish popular ballads." It is to her small niece, who was present at the first interview, and who was too young to have eaten from the tree of the knowledge of good and evil, that my thanks are due for the old ballad which I shall presently offer. This helpful innocent supplemented my rather indefinite requests by a suggestion that her aunt should sing "the song about the lady that killed her two babies," whereat she was hastily informed that there was no such song, and was further requested not to open her meddlesome mouth again. I boldly seconded the niece's entreaties, and extorted the admission that there was such a song, entitled "The Greenwood Siding," but was assured that it was incredibly foolish, that it was far from being respectable, and that nobody would be offended sooner than myself if it were sung in my presence. In the course of the argument which followed, however, Ellen graciously allowed herself to be persuaded that I was a person not easily offended, and this conclusion was prologue to the following version of "The Cruel Mother," rendered in a subdued minor key:

There was a lady came from York.
Down alone in the lonely
She fell in love with her father's clerk.
Down alone by the greenwood siding

She loved him well, she loved him long,
Down alone in the lonely
Till at length this young maid with child she
did prove.
Down alone by the greenwood siding

She leaned her back against an oak,
Down alone in the lonely
When first it bowed and then it broke.
Down alone by the greenwood siding

She leaned herself against a thorn,
Down alone in the lonely
And then her two babes they were born.
Down alone by the greenwood siding

She took her pen-knife keen and sharp,
Down alone in the lonely
And she pierced it through their innocent
hearts.
Down alone by the greenwood siding

She dug a hole seven feet deep.
Down alone in the lonely
She threw them in and bid them sleep.
Down alone by the greenwood siding

It's when this young maid was returning
home
Down alone in the lonely
She saw two babes a-playing ball.
Down alone by the greenwood siding

"O babes, O babes, if you were mine,
  Down alone in the lonely
I would dress you up in silks so fine."
Down alone by the greenwood siding

"O mother, O mother, when we were thine
  Down alone in the lonely
You did not dress us in silks so fine.
Down alone by the greenwood siding

"But you took your pen-knife keen and sharp,
  Down alone in the lonely
And you pierced it through our innocent
    hearts.
Down alone by the greenwood siding

"You dug a hole seven feet deep.
  Down alone in the lonely
You threw us in and bid us sleep."
Down alone by the greenwood siding

"O babes, O babes, what shall I do
  Down alone in the lonely
For the wicked crime I have done unto you?"
Down alone by the greenwood siding

"O mother, O mother, it's us can tell,
  Down alone in the lonely
For it's seven long years you shall ring a bell,
Down alone by the greenwood siding

"And seven more like an owl in the woods,
  Down alone in the lonely
And seven more like a whale in the sea.
Down alone by the greenwood siding

"The rest of your time you shall be in hell,
    Down alone in the lonely
And it's there you'll be fixed for eternity."
Down alone by the greenwood siding

When the singing was concluded I hastened to express my satisfaction, laying heavy stress upon the mellow antiquity of the ballad. But Isaac's Ellen was inclined to be sardonic. The story, she vehemently suspected, was an out-and-out lie. There might be such things as ghosts, to be sure, and we all knew that there were plenty of people who believed in them; but when it came to a game of ball and a long sermon from the ghosts of two babies it was quite evident that the person who made up the lie was going a little too far. Furthermore, if the song was an old one it seemed rather queer that it should be about a place called the Greenwood Siding. Railroads were started not so very long ago, and the siding, as every educated person knew, was a part of the railroad.

I took no bold stand on these abstruse matters, but made haste to copy the ballad and shelter it in my inside pocket from the devastating blast of Ellen's higher criticism. It was quite plain that Ellen had become modernized beyond the limits within which a singer must keep if he is to be an effective perpetuator of tradition. If ballads are to be kept alive they must be sung by believers to believers. The least breath of scepticism or of condescension is fatal; and while the sceptic may memorize a ballad as an interesting curiosity or copy it down as a significant relic, he cannot nourish it in a soil where it will continue to grow and develop as it has done in the past. I myself regard all popular ballads with affectionate admiration, but since I cannot accept the tale of the ghosts with conviction I am even less fitted to perpetuate "The Greenwood Siding" as a popular tradition than was Ellen, who had not entirely shaken herself free from the shackles of belief. Most of the singers whom I have presented in these pages were simple old men and women who not only loved and admired their ballads, but who sang in the unquestioning belief that they were detailing faithful records of actual events; and of such people is composed the slender link between the collector and the unrecorded traditions of the past. It seems to me to be of great significance that, out of the scores of ballads which I have heard at various times, no other one has been thus subjected by the singer to the fierce light of rational inquiry. And, as I have shown, it was only by a lucky accident that I was enabled to hear Ellen's singing of "The Greenwood Siding." My firm belief, then, is that ballad-singers—who are of an entirely different race from other singers—perpetuate only those ballads which from their point of view are trustworthy records of actual and important happenings, couched in language that is fitting and effective. If Ellen had been absolutely certain that "The Greenwood Siding" was an imposture she would probably not have sung it even to her small and credulous niece.

The next "English and Scottish popular ballad" which I shall present received its full meed of admiration and confidence from the old man who sang it to me. The ballad is a version of "Captain Wedderburn's Courtship," and the singer was John Adamson, a hale and vigorous youth of eighty-five, who in his day had mightily wielded the lumberman's axe, and as mightily had striven with any ballad-singer who had cared to match him, song for song. One of his stoutest allies in these stirring times was the merry and resourceful Captain whose courtship animates the following tale:

> The Duke of Merchant's daughter walked out one
>   summer's day.
> She met a bold sea-captain by chance upon the way.
> He says, "My pretty fair maid, if it wasn't for the law
> I would have you in my bed this night by either stock
>   or wa'."
>
> She sighed and said, "Young man, oh, do not me
>   perplex.
>
> .   .   .   .   .
>
> You must answer me in questions six before that I
>   gang awa'.
> Or before that I lie in your bed by either stock or wa'.
>
> "O what is rounder than your ring ? What's higher
>   than the trees?
> Or what is worse than woman's tongue?   What's
>   deeper than the seas?
> What bird sings first, what bird sings last?   Or where
>   does the dew first fall?—
> Before that I lie in your bed by either stock or wall."
>
> "The globe is rounder than your ring. Sky's higher
>   than the trees.
> The devil's worse than woman's tongue.   Hell's
>   deeper than the seas.
> The roe sings first, the thirst sings last. On the earth
>   the dew first falls,
> So you and I lie in one bed, and you lie next the
>   wall."

"You must get for me some winter fruit which in December grew.
You must get for me a silken cloak that ne'er a waft went through,
A sparrow's thorn, a priest new-born, before that I gang awa',
Before that I lie in your bed by either stock or wa'."

"My father's got some winter fruit which in December grew.
My mother's got a silken cloak that ne'er a waft went through.
Sparrow's thorns they're easy found. There's one on every claw.
So you and I lie in one bed and you lie next the wa'."

"You must get for my wedding supper a chicken without a bone.
You must get for my wedding supper a cherry without a stone.
You must get for me a gentle bird, a bird without a gall,
Before that I lie in your bed by either stock or wall."

"O when the chicken's in the egg I'm sure it has no bone.
And when the cherry's in full bloom I'm sure it has no stone.
The dove it is a gentle bird. It flies without a gall,
So you and I lie in one bed and you lie next the wall."

He took her by the lily-white hand and led her through the hall.

He held her by the slender waist for fear that she
    would fall.
He led her on his bed of down without a doubt at all.
So he and she lies in one bed, and he lies next the wall.

"He rolled over," explained old John in thunderous
tones. "That's what it means.—She was a smart gyurl,"
he added reflectively, "with her riddles an' her puzzles.
But she wasn't as smart as him. She met her match when
she run across the captain."

This song, John explained, was called "Six Questions,"
and here his explanation ended. I pressed him for information concerning the history and currency of the ballad,
but these antiquarian matters were of no interest to him.
He had learned it, countless years ago, from his wife, who
was no mean singer herself. His wife had learned it
"from a friend," and there the "Six Questions" disappeared in the mist. But the song was a good song and a
true, and what more did one need to know?

The "Six Questions" I procured on one of my excursions in the hilly region which lies back from the north
shore of Nova Scotia. My next find was made on the sea-
coast, in the heart of the district that I was using as a base
of operations.

One morning I strolled through a hayfield to where old
Sandy Rogers was sitting upon the horse-rake and shout-
ing orders to his patient beast with the air of robust indignation which is assumed, as a matter of etiquette, by all
men who labor with horses. Sandy, when under the influence of a softer mood, had been overheard by one of my
spies in the process of trolling an old and unfamiliar ditty
as he was driving in to the barn one evening. He was a

man-of-all-work or a devotee of slothful ease according to the exigencies or opportunities of the season, and he fished, shingled barns, worked at the crops, or reposed upon the lap of his dooryard, with equal mind. On the day in question he was helping one of the farmers to garner his hay, and as I approached he reined in his horse with a solemn and portentous air to pass the time of day with me.

"I could sing onct," admitted Sandy, while he thoughtfully extracted a black fig of Pictou twist from the pocket of his overalls, "but nobody ever wants to hear them old songs now." A vague suspicion knotted his forehead. "What on airth do you want to write them down for," he demanded,—"a great scholar like you, that's got he's house full o' books about hist'ry and portry?" I labored to convince Sandy that I was not above taking an interest in old-fashioned things even if other people were, and finally got his promise to think up as many old songs as he could and to sing them for me on the first day that was too wet to "work at the hayin'."

Two or three days after this the wind swung round to the northeast, driving in the heavy, stolid mass of black cloud that I was awaiting to summon me to the fireside of Sandy. "Well," roared my prospective entertainer when I had responded to this summons, "a nice mess I ben makin' o' the hay since I was talkin' to ye! I'd start me horse an' git goin' on one o' them blame old songs, an' the first thing I know I'd be half-way down the field with me hay scattered hell west an' crooked!" I made haste to assure Sandy that, in my opinion, the cause had fully justified the havoc that had been wrought upon the windrows, since the neglected hay was a crop that could be renewed year by year, while the precious ballads which were garnered in

111

his memory had been gleaned from a soil which could never again yield this kind of fruit in its season.

Sandy was inclined, on the whole, to sympathize with this point of view, and under its influence he soon went vigorously to work. He had several ballads of the sea, of the wars, and of the loves of young men and maidens; and each, as its turn came, was delivered in tones that caused the frail walls and the loosened windows of his cottage to shake with dread. Finally he seized upon one which almost immediately broke away from him. With a terrific clearing of the throat he grasped at it again:

> In India lived a noble lord—
> He's riches wuz beyond compare,

Once more the coy ballad eluded him and disappeared.

"Dang it!" roared Sandy. "I can't think of it while I'm settin' back in me chair. If I was out on the rake, drivin' up and down the field, I'd blame soon give it to ye." He suddenly leaped to his feet. "You set still fer a minute," he commanded, and rushed out into the yard.

I peered cautiously through the window, and beheld a stirring spectacle. Sandy was marching resolutely up and down the yard, with arms waving and hair and beard tossing wildly in the nor'east gale. His lips worked spasmodically, and at times a bellowed word or syllable came driving in through the rattling panes. Presently he made a rush for the door, and I had barely time to resume my seat and replace my pipe when he hurtled himself through the room, flung himself into his chair, and broke into a raging and irresistible torrent of song.

The ballad which was thus resolutely hunted down and

securely fettered was the old Scotch ballad which has appeared at various times and in various places as "Young Beichan," "Young Bicham," "Lord Bacon," and "Lord Bateman," to mention a few of its more familiar captions. The last-mentioned title was the one employed by Sandy, and the one, therefore, which had been current in this district in the days when the ballad had lived, moved, and had its being.

Some parts of Sandy's version were suspiciously incoherent, and this he himself was quite ready to admit. His suggestion was that I should look up his elder brother Dave, who used to sing the song in days gone by, and who could now be found in a village about twenty miles away. Towards Dave, then, I set my course a day or two after my visit to Sandy.

Both Dave and Sandy had vigorously survived the allotted period of the life of man, but Dave still held the superior and somewhat contemptuous attitude towards a relatively youthful and ignorant brother which had been the conventional relation of their earlier days. "What!" exclaimed Dave with scorn, when I told him of Sandy's recital of "Lord Bateman," "did Sandy try to make ye believe that he knowed that song? Well, I'm jist very *doubtful* if Sandy knowed it. I'm *very* doubtful if he knowed it. There used to be two people that could sing that song an' sing it right. One o' them was me father an' one was me, an' me father's been dead now for close onto seventeen year."

It was doubtless owing to Dave's unwillingness to enter into a mere competition with the youthful and erratic Sandy that he refused to sing the ballad at this stage. "You go ahead," he commanded, "an' read it the way

113

Sandy give it to ye, an' I'll let ye know when he's got it wrong." I therefore proceeded with the first and second stanzas, and at the conclusion of each Dave judicially signified approval with the remark, "He's heard me sing it often enough to git that part right." Then I read the third stanza:

> He sailèd east and he sailèd west,
>   Until he came to a Turkish shore.
> There he was taken and put in prison,
>   And bound down in irons strong.

Dave's upraised hand brought me to a sudden halt. "Sandy thought," said Dave bitterly, "that he could sing 'Lord Bateman' for ye, did he? Do ye know how that verse goes, when it's sung right?" Dave closed his eyes and tunefully made answer to himself:

> He sailèd east and he sailèd west,
>   Until he came to a Turkish shore.
> There he was taken and put in prison,
>   Where he could neither see nor hear.

In such fashion we proceeded through the ballad, at every step observing the most extreme caution. Sometimes Dave yielded to Sandy a grudging approval, and sometimes he convicted him of enormous crimes against truth, correctness, rhyme, and metre. The resultant ballad, which I shall now present, is as a matter of fact not very different from the original version which I procured from the much-berated Sandy:

In India lived a noble lord.
  His riches was beyond compare.
He was the darling of his parents,
  Of their estate the only heir.

In India lived a noble lord.
  His riches was beyond compare.
And yet he could never be contented
  Until a voyage he took to sea.

He sailèd east and he sailèd west,
  Until he came to a Turkish shore.
There he was taken and put in prison,
  Where he could neither see nor hear.

For seven long months he lay lamenting,
  He lay lamenting in irons strong,
Till he chanced to see the brisk young lady
  Who set him free from his prison chains.

The gaoler had one only daughter.
  A brisk young lady gay was she.
As she was passing the prison door
  She chanced Lord Bateman for to see.
She stole the keys of her father's prison,
  And opened it without delay.

"Have you got gold, and have you got silver?
  Have you got houses of high degree?
And what would you give to a fair lady
  If she from bondage would set you free?"

"Yes, I've got gold, and I've got silver,
  And I've got houses of high degree,
And all I'd give to a fair lady
  If she from bondage would set me free."

"It's not your gold, nor yet your silver,
　Nor yet your houses of high degree.
All that I want to make me happy,
　All that I crave is your fair body.

"Let's make a bargain and make it strong,
　For seven long years that it may stand,
That you will wed with no other woman,
　And me to wed with no other man."

When seven long years were gone and past,
　When seven long years were at an end,
She packèd up her richest clothing,
　Saying, "Now I'll go and seek my friend."

She sailèd east and she sailèd west
　Until she came to an Indian shore.
It's there she could not be contented.
　All for her true love she did inquire.

She inquired for Lord Bateman's palace
　At every corner of the street.
She inquired for Lord Bateman's palace
　Of every person she chanced to meet.

And when she came to Lord Bateman's palace
　She knocked so loudly on the ring,
And none was so ready as the brisk young
　　porter,
　To rise and let this young lady in.

She asked, "Is this Lord Bateman's palace?
　Or is the lord himself within?"
"O yes, O yes," said the brisk young porter,
　"He and his new bride has just come in."

116

She wept, she wept and wrung her hands,
  Crying, "Alas, I am undone!
I wish I was in my native country
  Across the seas there to remain.

"Go tell him to send me one ounce of bread
  And one bottle of his wine so strong,
And ask him if he's forgot the lady
  That set him free from his prison strong."

The porter went unto his master
  And kneelèd low down on his knees.
"Arise, arise, my brisk young porter,
  And tell me what the matter is."

"There is a fair lady stands at your gate,
  And she doth weep most bitterly.
I think she is the finest creature
  That I ever wish my eyes to see.

"She's got more rings on her forefinger,
  Around her waist she wears diamond strings,
She's got more gold about her clothing
  Than your new bride and all her kin.

"She wants you to send her one ounce of bread,
  One bottle of your wine so strong.
She wants me to ask if you've forgot the lady
  That set you free from your prison strong."

He stamped his foot upon the floor.
  He broke the table in pieces three,
Saying, "Adieu, adieu to my new wedded bride,
  For this fair lady I'll go and see."

It's up and steps the new bride's mother,
  And she was a lady of high degree,
Saying, "You have married my only daughter."
  "Well, she is none the worse of me.

"Since my fair one has arrived
  A second wedding there shall be.
Your daughter came on a horse and saddle,
  She shall go home on a coach and three."

He took this lady by the hand,
  He led her over the marble stones,
He changed her name from Susanna fair,
  And now she's the wife of Lord Bateman.

He took her by the lily-white hand,
  He led her through from room to room,
He changed her name from Susanna fair,
  And now she's the wife of Lord Bateman.

My discussion of the Nova Scotian versions of the old English and Scottish ballads is beginning to exhibit signs of plethora, but it must be still further expanded to include a very interesting version of "Young Johnson." This is not, so far as I can discover, one of the ballads that were widely current in the good old singing days, but it used to be sung by a favored few, and one of these few was John Thomas Matheson. John Thomas himself made this incautious admission to me one afternoon, and for many a day after he most bitterly regretted his indiscretion. He had, to be sure, sung ballads in the early days of his thoughtless youth, but even then he had been interested in his function of entertainer rather than in the intrinsic merit of his songs, and the intervening years which knew not the ballads had pretty thoroughly crowded out the recollection of them from his mind.

Furthermore, John Thomas was a procrastinator, not of the domestic garden variety, but of a rare and splendid orchid-like species hard to find even in this world of delays. He was, to speak allegorically, procrastination itself personified and incarnate. When I called on him I executed the final steps of my journey over a narrow, swaying board that had been placed to connect the framework for the floor of a porch which he had begun six years before, and which he was still daily planning to complete. And I have known him, after a week of comparative leisure, to light his lantern at eleven o'clock on Saturday night and proceed to the urgent business of shingling his barn, rejoicing in the inward assurance that the stroke of twelve would usher in the holy Sabbath, when we must neither work nor play.

Thus it may be seen that I had made no appreciable progress towards the capture of "Young Johnson" when I extorted from John Thomas the admission that he might be able to think up a few verses if he were given his time. With most singers this is the formal prelude to an almost immediate rendition of the ballad in question, but, coming from John Thomas, it had no more significance than a tale told by an idiot. The sight of a palpable and business-like pad of writing-paper filled him with a vague but unendurable alarm, and I might have had to resign the ballad definitely if I had not chanced by luck to hit upon the only device that would, in all probability, ever have proved successful.

A little distance up the road from John Thomas's unfinished home and imperfectly shingled barn lived a schoolgirl who had found special favor in the sight of the old man, and she cheerfully and confidently guaranteed to procure the ballad for me if I would leave the whole matter of negotiations to her. Consequently, when John Thomas looked hopefully across the road one morning for his usual greeting from his young friend he was met with a request for a song named "Young Johnson," and the following morning, when he was reassuring himself that he had cunningly disposed of the whole matter, he was asked to name the hour after school at which he could most conveniently repeat the song. Day in and day out my accomplice reminded him of the song as Desdemona reminded Othello of the suit of Michael Cassio, and partly through despair at the prospect of an endless persecution and partly through a kindly desire to win approbation from the child whom he delighted to honor, he finally repeated the following version, which was triumphantly copied out and delivered to me by my ally:

> As Johnson and the young Colonel
>   Together were drinking wine
> Says Johnson to the young Colonel,
>   "If you'll marry my sister, I'll marry thine."
>
> "No, I'll not marry your sister,
>   Nor shall you marry mine.
> For I will keep her for a miss
>   As I go through the town."
>
> Young Johnson has drawn his broad bright
>   sword
>   Which hung low down to the ground,
> And he has given the young Colonel
>   A deep and a deadly wound.

Then mounting on his milk-white steed
  He swiftly rode away
Until he came to his sister's house
  Long, long ere the break of day.

"Alight, alight, young Johnson," she said,
  "And take a silent sleep.
For you have crossed the stormy waters
  Which are both wide and deep."

"I cannot light, I cannot light,
  Nor neither sleep can I.
For I have killed the young Colonel,
  And for it I did fly."

"Oh have you killed the young Colonel?
  Oh woe be unto thee!
Tomorrow's morn at eight o'clock
  It's hangèd you shall be."

"O hold your tongue, you cruel woman,
  O hold your tongue," said he.
"How can I trust to a strange lady
  If I cannot trust to thee?"

He's mounted on his nimble steed,
  And swiftly rode away
Until he came to his own true love's
  Long, long ere the break of day.

"Alight, alight, young Johnson," she said,
  "And take a silent sleep.
For you have crossed the stormy waters
  Which are both wide and deep."

"I can't alight, I cannot stop,
  Nor neither sleep can I.
For I have killed the young Colonel
  And for it I must fly."

"Oh have you killed my brother?" she said,
  "Oh what shall now be done?
But come into my chamber,
  I'll secure you from all harm."

She's lockèd up his hawks,
  And she's lockèd up his hounds.
And she's lockèd by the nimble steed
  That bore him from the ground.

She's lockèd one, she's lockèd two,
  She's lockèd three or four.
And then she stood for his life guard
  Behind the empty door.

On looking east and looking west
  She happened for to see
Four and twenty of the King's Life-Guards
  Come riding merrily.

"O did you see young Johnson?" they said,
  "Or did he pass by this way?
For he has killed the young Colonel,
  And for it he did fly."

"What color was his hawk?" she said,
  "And what color was his hound?
And what color was the nimble steed
  That bore him from the ground?"

"A dark grey was his hawk," they said,
　"And a light grey was his hound.
And a milk-white was the nimble steed
　That bore him from the ground."

"Then ride away, O ride away,
　And quickly ride, I pray.
Or I fear he'll be out of London town
　Long, long ere the dawn of day."

She went into his chamber
　For to tell him what she had done.
And he has pierced his lovely dear
　That ne'er did him any wrong.

Young Johnson, being in a silent sleep,
　And dreaming they were near,
He has drawn his bright broad sword
　And pierced his lovely dear.

"What cause for this, dear Johnson?" she said,
　O what is this you've done?
For you have pierced your dearest dear
　That ne'er did you any wrong."

"O can you live?　O can you live?
　Can you live but one single half-hour?
And all the doctors in London town
　Shall be within your bower."

"I cannot live.　I cannot live.
　O how can I live?" said she.
"For don't you see my very heart's blood
　Come trickling down from my knee?

"O ride away, you ride away,
   And quickly get over the plain.
And never let it once enter your mind
   That your own true love you've slain."

Several other versions of the old traditional ballads I have heard of, or myself have heard in the days when I was still privileged to sit in the bodily presence of old Ned Langille. I have not ceased to cherish the hope that I may yet extort from some crafty singer the admission that he knows "a line or two" of "James Harris" or of "Bolender Martin," but so far I have had to content myself with the certain but unsatisfying knowledge that both of these ballads were once current in the northern part of Nova Scotia. One other ballad of century-old traditional character I have obtained, and with its presentation I shall incontinently conclude this drawn-out chapter. It is a version, corrupted by "elegant" additions from the eighteenth century, of the ballad of "Fair Margaret and Sweet William," and it was copied down for me by one of my college friends from a recitation by his mother.

As Margaret was in her pretty bouree
   A-combing her locks so fair,
She saw the rich wedding of William go by
   Which struck her to the heart.

"O mother, come quickly, come bind up my
     head,
   O sister, come make up my bed.
For I have a pain that lies at my heart
   That will bring me to my grave."

Her mother she quickly came bound up her
    head,
    Her sister she made up her bed.
And she had a pain that lay at her heart
    That brought her to her grave.

In the middle of the night, about twelve o'clock,
    All people in bed and asleep,
The ghost of Margaret rose up again,
    And stood at William's bed feet.

"O how do you like your pillow?" she said,
    "And how do you like your sleep?
And how do you like your widow lady
    That sleeps in your arms so sweet?"

"Well do I like my pillow," he said,
    "And well do I like my sleep.
But ten thousand times better do I like the
    ghost
    That stands at my bed feet."

Then William he quickly jumped up out of
    bed,
    And ran to Margaret's hall.
There's none so ready as Margaret's mother
    To answer William's night call.

"Is Margaret in her pretty bouree,
    Or is she in the hall?"
"She is laid out in a long white robe
    With her lips as cold as clay."

The Quest of the Ballad

He kissed her once, he kissed her twice,
 He kissed her three times o'er.
He made an oath, a solemn oath,
 And never kissed woman more.

Margaret died on one good day,
 And William died on the morrow.
Margaret died with a heart full of love,
 And William died for sorrow.

Margaret was buried at the chancel gate,
 And William was buried at the choir.
Out of Margaret's grave grew a beautiful rose,
 Out of William's there grew a sweet briar.

The rose grew tall and the sweet-briar too,
 Till they could grow no higher,
They twined together in a true lovers' knot,
 The rose wrapped around the sweet briar.

CHAPTER SEVEN

TYPES OF CURRENT BALLADS

I should now like to present a sort of rough classification of the ballads which I have gathered from time to time and in various parts of Nova Scotia. No classification, to be sure, could be consistent or inclusive. Some ballads arrange themselves in groups and others remain austerely apart, preferring the distinction that belongs to individuality or eccentricity. And even where groups are formed the nature of the grouping is sometimes of one kind, sometimes of another, so that it is impossible to build up a classification on any single or consistent basis. But in discussing ballads, as in discussing men, one may gain something by generalizing and by citing typical examples from various groups, even though one's discussion should be so inconsequential as to pass from ghost ballads to ballads with a refrain and from thence to ballads composed in America. My chief object in thus generalizing is to indicate roughly the main varieties of ballads that are now current, since my own collection is fairly typical.

First in importance are such versions of the genuine old popular ballads as I have presented in the last chapter. These are now of the greatest rarity in any district, and are more precious than jewels and gold. Many of the very finest examples of the old stock were in the possession of the early settlers on the north shore of Nova Scotia, and some of them, as we have seen, were passed down from father to son even unto the generation which is now distinguished by the withered cheek and the shuffling gait. Farther than this they have shown no disposition to advance; and I regard myself with a glow of complacency when I reflect that, if I had not played the knight-errant in the nick of time, many of them, as matters of Nova Scotia tradition, would now be resting in the quiet grave with those who sang them. On the other hand sits the mournful reflection that if I had started out earlier I should have procured more. The addition of even one year at the beginning of my work would have put me in possession of the complete stock of Little Ned Langille. But that way madness lies. No more of that!

Since I have pretty thoroughly discussed these older ballads I may now proceed to a closely related and equally arbitrary division. Several ballads of a much later generation are composed upon old traditional themes. A few such I have collected in Nova Scotia. In one or two of them the resemblance to older ballads is so close as to be, pretty obviously, the resemblance between child and parent; in others the similarity may be merely accidental, if one can ever call accidental the recurrence of a motive which has a profound and perennial appeal for men. A comparison between these ballads and their prototypes yields only one general conclusion: ballads are like wine, and the old is better than the new.

But all new wine is not alike bad, and I have in my collection one song, "The Sea-Captain," which is not unworthy to be placed beside its mellow forefather ballad, "The Broomfield Hill,"—itself a version of a theme common to romance, tale, and legend, and almost as old and as widespread as the earth we tread on. The theme is that of the maiden who is lured into the power of a lover, but who exercises her nimble wits to such good effect—sometimes employing magic and sometimes lulling the wooer to sleep—that she is presently enabled to escape unsullied and unharmed. This theme is thus treated in "The Sea-Captain," a ballad as bright and attractive as the resourceful maiden herself:

It was of a sea captain that followed the sea,
    Let the winds blow high or blow low O.
"I shall die, I shall die," the sea captain did cry,
    "If I don't get that maid on the shore O."

This captain had jewels, this captain had gold,
    This captain had costly a ware O.
And all he would give to this pretty fair maid
    If she'd please take a sail from the shore O.

With great persuasions they got her on board,
    The weather being fine and clear O.
She sang so sweet, so neat and complete,
    That she sang all the seamen to sleep O.

She took all his jewels, she took all his gold,
    She took all his costly a ware O.
She took his broad sword to make her an oar,
    And she paddled her way to the shore O.

"O were my men mad or were my men drunk,
    Or were my men deep in despair O,
To let her away with her beauty so gay,
    To roam all alone on the shore O,"

"Your men were not mad, your men were not drunk,
    Your men were not deep in despair O.
I deluded your men as well as yourself,
    I'm a maid again on the shore O."

The other ballad which I shall select from this class has
little to recommend it beyond its fine adaptability as an
illustration of the rule that the old is better. In a previous
chapter I have presented the Nova Scotia version of
"Lord Bateman," which, by means of a simple and apparently unimpassioned narrative, first moves us to love
and sympathy for the enamoured Turkish maiden, then
harrows us with suspense for the outcome of her piteous
attempts to find her lover, and finally enables us to throw
up our hats rejoicing that she will never again have to
sail the seas east and west. "The Turkish Lady," a more
modern ballad which apparently takes its starting-point
from "Lord Bateman," makes repeated rhetorical attempts
to enlist our sympathy and admiration, but succeeds only
in persuading us that the young man is a prig who would
not have deserved his good fortune but for the fact that a
substantial part of the fortune is a mere love-ridden and
vacillating lady whom he has met in Turkey. The ballad,
to be sure, would be well enough if it did not challenge the
fatal comparison with a much better one,—which will be
more evident, perhaps, if I permit it now to speak for
itself:

> Young virgins all, I pray draw near.
> A pretty story you shall hear.
> 'Twas of a Turkish lady brave
> That fell in love with an English slave.
>
> A merchant ship at Bristol lay
> As we were sailing o'er the sea.
> By a Turkish slaver took were we,
> And all of us made slaves to be.

They bound us down in irons strong.
They whipped and lashed us all along.
No tongue could tell, I'm certain sure,
What we poor seamen could endure.

Come set you down and listen a while,
And hear how fortune did on me smile.
It was my fortune for to be
A slave unto a rich lady.

She dressed herself in rich array,
And went to view her slaves one day.
Hearing the moan the young man made,
She went to him and thus she said:

"What countryman, young man, are you?"
"An Englishman, and that is true."
"I wish you were some Turk," said she,
"I would ease you of your misery.

"I'll ease you of your slavish work
If you'll consent and turn a Turk.
I'll own myself to be your wife,
For I do love you as my life."

"No, no," then said he,
"Your conscience slave, madam, I'll be.*
I'd sooner be burnt at a stake
Before that I'd my God forsake."

This lady to her chamber went
And spent her night in discontent.
Little Cupid with his piercing dart
Did deeply wound her to the heart.

* The first two lines of the stanza are, it is scarcely necessary to point out, incoherent; but the stanza is easily redeemed by the loud, clear, and determined rhetorical outburst of the remaining lines.

She was resolvèd the next day
To ease him of his slavery,
And own herself to be his wife,
For she did love him as her life.

She dressed herself in rich array,
And with the young man sailed away.
Unto her parents she bade adieu.
By this you see what love can do.

A very large and important division of the ballads now
current is the one presenting variations of the following
motive: A traveller, newly arrived in the country, approaches a maiden, and, with apparently indecent haste,
makes proposals for her hand. The maiden rejects him
with scorn, remarking that she has, in some foreign land
or out upon the seas, a lover to whom she will remain
faithful until he comes to claim her. The stranger makes
repeated and unsuccessful attempts to shake her faith in
the absent one, but at last produces half of a gold ring,
proving that he himself is the long-absent lover, who, years
before, divided a ring with this identical maiden in token
of betrothal. Just why the returned lover should thus
prolong the delicious moment of recognition is not always
clear. From his point of view the conversation may be
simply a revelling in the joys of artificial suspense, or a
somewhat dubious method of breaking the news of his return. It always, however, produces the same constant effect upon the ballad-singer's audience, which is transported with admiration for the unwavering fidelity of the
maiden to her plighted troth.

A fair example of this class is the following untitled
ballad:

As a maid was walking in her garden
  A single sailor came riding by.
He stepped up to her, he thought he knew her,
  He said, "Fair maid, can you fancy I?"

"You appear to me like some man of honor,
  Like some noble lord you appear to me.
How can you impose on a poor young creature
  Who is not fitted your servant to be?"

"If you're not fitted to be my servant,
  I have some great reward for thee.
I'll marry you, I'll make you my lady,
  And I'll have servants to wait on thee."

"I have a true love all of my own, sir,
  And it's seven long years he's been to sea,
And it's seven long years I'll wait upon him.
  If he's alive he'll return to me."

"How can you fancy a roving sailor?
  How can you fancy such a slave?
He may be dead in some foreign country,
  Or else the ocean has proved his grave."

"If he's alive I'll hope to see him,
  And if he's dead I hope he's blest;
'Tis for his sake I'll never marry,
  For he's the one that I love best."

"Such a girl as you I do admire,
  Such a girl as you to be my bride.
You shall have gold and silver plenty,
  And treasures flowing on every side."

"O what care I for your gold and silver?
  O what care I for your birth and land?
O what care I for your old maid-servant
  If my own sailor returns to me?"

He slipped his hand into his pocket.
  His fingers were both slim and small.
He pulled out a ring that was broken between them.
  Soon as she seen it she down did fall.

He picked her up into his arms,
  And kisses he gave her, one, two by three,
Saying, "I am your young and your single sailor.
  I've just returned to marry thee."

"If you're my true and my single sailor
  Your shape and color do not agree.
But seven years makes a great alteration,
  And sure there's seven since I did you see."

To church they went and they both got married
  With their two hearts full of love and content.
He stays at home and takes his ease,
  And he goes no more on the raging seas.

I have collected, at various times, about a score of ballads of this class, and each one presents a slightly varied form of the animating motive. Sometimes the lover has been at sea, sometimes in the army, sometimes in foreign lands carving out his fortunes, and in one case he has been through the Napoleonic wars and has just returned from the Battle of Waterloo. The arguments by which he tests the faith of the maiden are also varied. In the ballad just presented he merely resorts to the conjecture that the absent lover is dead or unfaithful; but often he goes a step further and affirms that he knew the lover, and either witnessed his death or else beheld him revelling in the charms of a new mistress. Usually, also, an attempt is made to impart an air of verisimilitude to the situation by providing some sort of natural disguise for the returned lover, since he could hardly expect to confront his old sweetheart in broad daylight and in the same figure in which he had formerly associated with her. Sometimes he speaks from behind the mask of night, and sometimes, as in the ballad just given, he has grown stouter and browner during the intervening years. Under cover of one of these disguises he confidently pursues his conversation with the sorely tried maiden, who frequently weeps, and sometimes faints, but who remains steadfast in the face of every inducement to do otherwise, and in the end is always rewarded by seeing the apparent stranger transformed into the actual lover.

Another very prevalent motive, in the ballads which I have met, is that of the maiden who wishes to clothe herself in men's attire and accompany her lover to sea or to the wars. In some cases the ballad is taken up with the arguments of the two lovers on this topic, and in others the maiden allows her sweetheart to go on his way, then quietly dons her masculine disguise and follows him. The sample which I shall now present is of the argumentative sort:

'Twas in one summer season, the twentieth of May,
We hoisted our English colors and we did make for sea.
The sun did shine most glorious. To Lisbon we were
    bound.
The hills and dales were covered with pretty maids all
    round.

I spied a handsome sailor just in his blooming years

.   .   .   .   .

Just coming to his true love to let her understand
That he was going to leave her and sail for some foreign
  land.

"The King has wrote for seamen, and I for one must go,
And for my very life, my love, I dare not answer no."
"Oh stay at home, dear Willie, and I will be your wife,
For the parting with you, Willie, is the parting of my
  life."

"But if I was to stay at home another would take my place.
And that would be a shame for me, likewise a sad dis-
  grace."
"My yellow hair I will cut off, men's clothing I'll put on.
I'll be thy body-servant, likewise thy waiting-man."

"Thy waist it is too slender, love, thy fingers are too small
To wait on me in battle where many a man does fall,
Where cannon they do rattle and bullets they do fly,
And silver trumpets they do sound to drown the dismal
  cries."

"My yellow hair I will cut off, men's clothing I'll put on.
No storms or dangers do I fear, let the winds blow high or
  low."
"But if I was to meet some other in sweeter charms than
  thee,
And she was to please my fancy, what would my Nancy
  say?"

"What would I say, dear Willie? and I would love her too,
And I would gently step aside while she would be talking
  to you."

"Dear Nancy, all these words are enough to break my
    heart.
Pray let us then be married before that we depart."

Now this young couple's married and they sail o'er the
    main.
I hope good luck may attend them till they return again.

In this ballad the lover and his mistress depart together
in the guise of two comrades; but far oftener the maiden
is left behind mourning, and she then adopts men's attire
before proceeding alone to seek her lover. But regularly
in this class of ballads, as in the one previously discussed,
the journeys end in lovers meeting,—with one tragic exception, the ballad of "Willie Taylor." In this rather
curious variation of a well-recognized ballad motive the
maiden reaches the end of her journey only to find her
faithless William in the company of a new mistress, and
she then promptly and ruthlessly slays him amid the
plaudits of the bystanders, and—it is worth noting—with
the complete approval of those who sing the ballad of her
adventures. The account of this episode, which is brief
and pithy, is as follows:

Willie Taylor, brisk young sailor, courted by a lady gay,
A day or two before the marriage pressed he was and sent
    away.
She dressed herself in men's attire, boldly entered for
    Jacky Tar.
Her lily-white hands and long slender fingers daubed they
    were with pitch and tar.

When she came to the field of battle there she stood
  amongst the rest.
A silver button flew off her waistcoat, there appeared her
  milk-white breast.
When the captain saw this wonder he said, "What wind
  has blown you here?"
"I am in search of my true love whom you pressed and I
  love dear."

"If you're in search of your true lover tell to me your
  true love's name."
"My true love's name is Willie Taylor whom you pressed
  to the Isle of Man."
"If your true love is William Taylor I find he is a false
  young man,
For he is to be married to-morrow to a lady of this land.

"If you rise early in the morning, early by the break of
  day,
There you'll see young Willie Taylor walking with his
  lady gay."
She rose early in the morning, early by the break of day,
And there she saw young Willie Taylor walking with his
  lady gay.

She called out for a sword and pistol, sword and pistol at
  her command,
And then she shot young Willie Taylor and his bride at
  his right hand.
When the captain saw this wonder he laughed loudly at
  the fun,
Saying, "You shall be captain and chief commander over
  my sailors every one."

If Willie Taylor was as constant a lover, as constant a
    lover as he could pretend,
She never would have been so cruel as her true love's days
    to end.

The districts where I have found most of my ballads
are on or near the sea-coast, and, as might be expected, the
collection has a very fair sprinkling of sea ballads. Some
of these are designed merely to show the dangers and de-
lights of life on the ocean, but most of them are of a more
sanguinary nature, instinct with the lust of battle, and
ringing with triumph for victory over the enemies of
Britain. I have three of these which present varying accounts of the mighty single combat between the Chesapeake and the Shannon, and each of the three singers
from whom I procured them gave me a solemn warning
not to sing them "in the States," as the inevitable result
of such boldness would be a thrashing at the hands of the
enraged American audience. This advice I have carefully
observed, not from any base fear of American reprisals,
but from an amply warranted conviction of my inability
to sing "in the States" or in any other country. But one
of the three ballads I feel that I can here present with
complete safety, in any case, since the only version of it
that I could find is incomplete, stopping short with a becoming delicacy and moderation while the victory still
hangs in the balance. The surviving portion runs thus:

'Twas of the Shannon frigate
    In the merry month of May;
To watch those bold Americans
    Off Boston light she lay.

THE QUEST OF THE BALLAD

The Chesapeake lying in harbor,
    A frigate stout and fine,
She had four hundred and sixty men
      on board,
    And her guns was forty-nine.

Captain Brooke he commanded us,
    A challenge he did write
To the captain of the Chesapeake
    To bring her out to fight.

He says, "My noble Lawrence,
    Don't think it's through enmity,
For it's to show to all the world
    That Britain rules the sea."

The challenge being accepted,
    The Chesapeake she bore down.
And she was as fine a frigate
    As belonged to the British crown.

Yard arm and broadside
    For a quarter of an hour,
When that enemy's ship drove up alongside,
    And her yard got locked in ours.

At this point the singer's memory flatly refused to work, and we were compelled to leave the two stout frigates with yards locked, in a state of perpetual mortal combat. But the ancient bard who sang the ballad was careful to warn me that I should not be lulled into a false sense of security by this circumstance. "If I was you," he said, "I wouldn't try to sing that one when I go back to the States. They know very well how the Chesapeake got licked, an' they

140

wouldn't thank ye fer puttin' them in mind of it.—I'll give ye one," he exclaimed presently, after a few minutes of anxious reflection, "that the Yankees'll like better than that one. It's about their great sea-captain that was named Paul Jones."

The song that followed was a brief but stirring account of how Paul Jones sailed from Baltimore in his frigate, "the Richard by name," and how he presently cleared the decks for an engagement with two British warships that hove in view. The cowardly ship's carpenter attempted to dissuade him by announcing that the ship was leaking like a basket, but the undaunted Paul "in the height of his pride" made the following answer:

"If we can't do no better let her sink alongside."

So they hove to and went at it, or, in the nobler language of the poet, who feigns himself to have been one of the crew,

We fought them four glasses, four glasses so hot,
Till fifty bold seamen lie dead on the spot,
And fifty-five wounded and bleeding in gore,
While the thundering loud cannons of Paul Jones
did roar.

The end, of course, is an unqualified victory for Paul Jones, who then invites his brave followers to "drink deep from the can" in honor of their country.

This is the only sea-ballad that I have found in which the enemies of Britain are generously allowed to bear away the victory. I have acquired considerable numbers from Bob Langille, Dick Hinds, and other less prolific singers, but in every other case the smoke of battle clears away to reveal the Union Jack flaunting itself above the high seas. Nelson's victory at Trafalgar is the theme of several rousing accounts, and some five or six deal with the Government operations against the pirates. Two of these are narratives of the combat which swept from the high seas the black flag of Kelly the Pirate, and the shorter of them I should like to present:

> Captain Cooper gave orders on the first of May
> To cruise in the Channel for our enemy—
> To protect our commerce from that daring foe
> And all our merchant ships where they would go.

Chorus.
> Then it's O Britons, stand true.
> Stand true to your colors, stand true.

> It was early one morning, to the wind we did lie,
> The man at the mast-head a sail he did spy.
> "A sail! O, a sail!" he loudly did cry,
> "She is a large cutter and seems to lay by."

> Our noble commander he pulled out his glass,
> So did our lieutenant to see what she was.
> Our captain stepped up and he viewed her all round,
> Says, "That's Kelly the Pirate, I'll bet fifty pound!

> "Don't you see that villain?" he cried, "Make sail!
> We'll soon overtake him, my boys, I'll give bail.
> Lay aloft, shake your reefs out, set everything clear,
> And up with your hellum and for him we'll steer."

We sailed till we came within gunshot.
Bold Kelly he seemed for to value us not.
With a loud voice like thunder Cooper did say,
"Load your guns, light your matches, and fire away!"

We engaged with that cutter four hours and more,
Till the blood from our scuppers like water did pour.
With round and grape metal we peppered his hull
Till down came his mizzenmast, colors and all.

We towed him in Portsmouth that very same day,
And then on to Newgate sent Kelly away.
Here's a health to our captain and officers too.
Here's a health to Stag frigate and all of her crew.

In this ballad all the sympathies are enlisted on the side
of law and order, and the luckless Kelly the Pirate is sent
on his way to the gallows without a sigh. Many of the
Nova Scotia ballads celebrate the adventures of highway-
men, and these, on the contrary, are always narrated from
the point of view of the sympathizer. Jack Shepard, Jack
Williams, and bold Jack Donahue are the heroes of a
thrilling series of tales in verse. In a previous chapter I
have presented the ballad which deals with the career of
Donahue, beginning at the time when "in Dublin city of
renown his first breath ever he drew," conducting him on
his enforced journey to Australia, and leaving him only at
the conclusion of his last gallant fight with the Sydney
constables, when

Nine rounds he fired and killed five men before the fatal
    ball
That pierced the heart of Donahue and caused him for to
    fall.

The adventures of Jack Shepard and Jack Williams are narrated more briefly; and equally condensed accounts are, in a few cases, accorded the young men and women who from time to time sallied forth upon the highway for sustenance or for revenge. But the hero of the road who appears most frequently is Dick Turpin, the notorious highwayman who, in the early part of the eighteenth century, persuaded so many luckless travellers to stand and deliver. He seems to have had a peculiar appeal for the popular imagination, and several legends of his adventurous career are still told by the superannuated. Last September I smoked my pipe one afternoon with a hale old countryman, in years eighty-seven strong, who in the intervals of ballad-singing regaled me with prose accounts of Dick Turpin, all of which, he said, were true. One of the Turpin ballads which he sang for me is brief enough to be repeated, and pithy enough to be worth repeating. It is entitled "Turpin and the Lawyer":

As Turpin was a riding across the moor,
There he saw a lawyer riding on before.
Turpin, riding up to him, said, "Are you not afraid
To meet Dick Turpin, that mischievous blade?"

Chorus.
Singing Eh ro, Turpin I ro.

Says Turpin to the lawyer for to be cute,
"I hid my money into my boot."
Says the lawyer to Turpin, "He can't find mine,
For I hid it in the cape of my coat behind."

They rode along together to the foot of the hill,
When Turpin bid the lawyer to stand still,
Saying, "The cape of your coat it must come off,
For my horse is in want of a new saddle-cloth."

Turpin robbed the lawyer of all his store.
He told him to go home and he would get more.
"And the very first town that you come in,
You can tell them you was robbed by Dick Turpin."

The old man who sang this ballad had also had his encounters with representatives of the law, and he had not emerged from them as happily as had his hero Dick Turpin. At the conclusion of the song, therefore, his face gleamed with a fury of demonic satisfaction as he smote his thigh and roared, "That was one time when a lawyer left somethin' behind him!"

"Dick Turpin and the Lawyer" belongs primarily to the category of Highwayman Ballads, where I have placed it, but it owes much of its effectiveness to the execution of a practical joke. This latter motive appears, also in a subordinate capacity, in many other ballads and in various categories. It appears regularly, for instance, in that large group in which the returned lover questions his sweetheart under the guise of a stranger. But here the situation is profoundly serious, and the grief and distress of the maiden are frequently so poignant as to be almost tragic. The feeling aroused in the listener is one of suspense and of sympathy for the maiden, and there is never the least tendency to regard the trick with humorous appreciation for its own sake. In another group of ballads, however, the effectiveness of the plot depends entirely upon the planning and executing of a practical joke by a person who is driven to defend or to vindicate himself, and who is heartily admired and applauded for his cleverness. Here the sympathy is all with the contriver of the joke, and the listener may with a free mind permit himself to roar and slap his knees at the discomfiture of the victim. There is the ballad of Zillah, who "on a certain day" disguises herself as a man, proceeds to the highway with a stout pair of pistols, and compels her lover to stand and deliver his watch and money. Here, however, intrudes a touch of sentiment: the lover flatly refuses to give up the diamond ring which, in this prophetic reversal of the positions of the sexes, he has received as a token from his true love, the pinchbeck highwayman, and the latter rides away much impressed by his devotion. There is also the ballad of the irate husband who returns home with the shrewd suspicion that Bill the Weaver has been courting his wife and is now concealed in the chimney, and who therefore proceeds with such enthusiasm to make his preparations for a roaring fire that the lurking Bill in abject terror finally decides to emerge and take his drubbing. But possibly the best example of this class is the ballad of "Kate and Her Horns," which tells how the resourceful Kate, by the simple expedient of scaring a young man into fits, transforms him from an inconstant lover into a tractable husband. This one I should like to present in full:

> You that in merriment delight,
> Pray listen now to what I write.
> So shall you satisfaction find,
> Will cure a melancholy mind.
>
> A damsel sweet in Colchester,
> And there a clothier courted her
> For three months' space, both night and day,
> But yet the damsel still said nay.

She said, "Were I to love inclined,
Perhaps you soon might change your mind
And court some other damsel fair,
For men are false, I do declare."

He many propositions made,
And like a royal lover said,
"There's none but you shall be my wife,
The joy and comfort of my life."

At length this maid gave her consent
To marry him, and straight they went
Unto their parents then, and woe,*
Both gave their leave and liking too.

But see the cursèd fruits of gold!
He left his royal love behind
With grief and love encompassed round,
Whilst he a greater fortune found.

A lawyer's daughter fair and bright,
Her parents' joy and whole delight,
He was resolved to make his spouse,
Denying all his former vows.

And when poor Kate she came to hear
That she must lose her only dear
All for the lawyer's daughter's sake,
Some sport of him Kate thought she'd make.

Kate knew when every night he came
From his new love, Nancy by name,
Sometimes at ten o'clock or more.
Kate to a tanner went, therefore,

* Possibly this should read "lo!"

147

And borrowed there an old cowhide
With crooked horns both large and wide,
And when she wrapped herself therein
Her new intrigue she did begin.

Kate to a lonesome field did stray.
At length the clothier came that way,
And he was sore ascared at her,
She looked so like old Lucifer.

A hairy hide, horns on her head,
Which near three feet asunder spread.
With that he saw a long black tail.
He strove to run, but his feet did fail.

And with a grum and doleful note,
She quickly seized him by the throat,
And said, "You'd leave poor Kate, I fear,
And hold a lawyer's daughter dear.

"Now since you've been so false to her,
You perjured knave of Colchester,
You shall, whether you will or no,
Into my gloomy regions go."

This voice did so affrighten him
He, kneeling on his trembling limbs,
Cried, "Master Devil, spare me now,
And I'll perform my former vow.

"I'll make young Kate my lawful bride."
"See that you do," the Devil cried.
"If Kate against you doth complain
Soon shall you hear from me again."

It's home he went, though very late.
He little thought that it was Kate
That put him into such a fright.
Therefore next day by morning light

He went to Kate and married her
For fear of that old Lucifer.
Kate's friends and parents thought it strange
That there was such a sudden change.

Kate never let her parents know,
Nor any other friend or foe,
Till they a year had married been,
She told it at her lying-in.

It pleased the women to the heart.
They said she fairly played her part.
Her husband laughed as well as they.
It was a joyful merry day.

The next category that occurs to me is the one including ballads which present the remorseful confessions of criminals,—a sufficiently abrupt transition from the merry ballads of the preceding class. In this new category the first person is employed throughout. Sometimes we find the narrator in prison for his crimes, but not in immediate danger of the extreme penalty, so that the preliminary explanation may assume some such form as this:

Seven long years I have laid in prison,
Seven more I've got to stay,
For knocking a man down in the alley
And stealing his greenbacks away.

THE QUEST OF THE BALLAD

But usually he is facing the unpleasant prospect of being
hanged by the neck until he is dead, in which case he most
lustily implores the Lord to have mercy on his soul, and
most heartily abases himself during the recital of his mis-
deeds.

I have one ballad of Nova Scotia origin which is a fine
example of this class. It is the last confession of Charles
Augustus Andersen, one of a group of mutineers who,
many years ago, were apprehended and sent to Halifax to
be hanged—all of which I shall relate in full in another
chapter. In this ballad the unhappy mutineer states, with
a lugubrious mixture of boldness and contrition:

> Charles Augustus Andersen is my right and proper
> name.
> Since I came to custody I ne'er denied the same.
> I came of honest parents although I die in scorn.
> Believe me, now I much lament that ever I was born.

Then he proceeds to relate the story of the mutiny in which
he was implicated, laying heavy stress on his own native
goodness of heart and on the baleful nature of the influence which was brought to bear upon him through the
counsels of older and wickeder men. Chief of these was
the scoundrel Fielding, who is introduced in the following
mournful stanzas:

> They shipped me on board the Saladin, as you will
> understand.
> She was bound for Valparaiso. Mackenzie had com-
> mand.
> We arrived there in safety without the least delay,
> Till Fielding came on board of her. Curse on that
> fatal day!

'Twas Fielding who induced us to do that horrid crime.
We might have prevented it if we had thought in time.
We shed the blood of innocents. The same I don't deny.
We stained our hands in human blood, for which we
    have to die.

Charles Augustus concludes his recital; then follow two stanzas describing with mingled grief and admiration the scene which put a period to this blighted career. "With his own hand," exclaims the poet,

With his own hand he greased the cord that cut the
    thread of life.

An even finer example of this class is "The Flying Cloud." This ballad narrates at great length the history of another possessor of the sinister name of Anderson, who is, however, related to Charles Augustus only in his unfortunate and entirely innocent predilection for being decoyed into the paths of crime. This victim of evil and designing companions is allowed to appropriate the ballad from beginning to end, and we are left to conclude for ourselves that when his song was ended he was led out to swing upon the gallows-tree. He begins with a cheerful confidence almost bordering on defiance:

My name it is Robert Anderson,
    I'd have you to understand.
I belong to the city of Waterford,
    Near Erin's happy land.

When I was young and in my prime,
    And health did on me smile,
My parents doted on me,
    I being their only child.

But gradually the tone grows bitter and despondent. Robert falls in with Captain Moore, a fiend in man's shape who invites him to ship on board his slave-trader, "The Flying Cloud." The transportation of slaves, as Robert unctuously describes it, is a tolerably brutal employment, but it is entirely too easy-going a life for Captain Moore, who presently comes out with a new suggestion for Robert and the other innocents on board his ship:

"There's gold and silver to be had
   If you with me remain.
We'll hist the lofty pirate flag
   And scour the Spanish Main."

To this of course we all agreed,
   Excepting five young men,
And two of them were Boston chaps,
   And two from Newfoundland.

The other was an Irishman
   Belonging to Trimore.
I wish to God I had joined those men
   And went with them on shore.

We robbed and plundered manys a ship
   Down on the Spanish Main,
Caused many a widow and orphan child
   In sorrow to remain.

Their crews we made them walk the plank,
   Caused them a watery grave,
For the saying of our captain was
   That a dead man tells no tales.

At last a gloomy day dawns upon The Flying Cloud. She is overtaken and captured by a Spanish man-o'war, her captain is killed, and her crew sent to Newgate to bide the journey to the gallows-tree. As we take our leave of poor misguided Robert he is awaiting the summons and bitterly cursing the evil influences that have conspired to bring him to this sorry pass:

> 'Tis drinking and bad company
> That made a wretch of me.
> Come all young men, think of my downfall,
> And curse to the pirate sea.

It is an easy transition from the "doleful matter" of the Confession Ballads to two closely related and equally lugubrious motifs which I shall now briefly notice. These are the Dream motif and the Avenging Ghost motif. I have, in my time, run across several examples of both of these melancholy types of song, and they are all alike in general character, that is, each of them relates the gruesome tale of a murder exposed through a supernatural agency. The only difference is that in one case this agency is a dream and in the other it is a ghost.

In the former class we have such ballads as "The Constant Farmer's Son," which was sung to me by old John Adamson in his little garden one bright summer morning when it seemed quite incredible that murders and murder-revealing dreams could ever find a place in a world so peaceful. Nevertheless, John assured me that the song was strictly true, and if he had been, like his companion, a pedant and not a jolly old ballad-singer, he could have called upon Boccaccio and John Keats to corroborate his

153

statement. For "The Constant Farmer's Son" is a popular version of a tale which was told nearly six hundred years ago in the Decameron, and which was expanded by Keats into the beautiful poetic narrative of "Isabella." It is the tale of the fair young woman of gentle birth who falls in love with a young man who is employed on her father's estate, and who starts up in bed one night from the dreadful and prophetic vision of her murdered lover:

As Mary on her pillow lay she dreamt a shocking dream.
She dreamt she saw her own true love down by a purling
 stream.
So Mary rose, put on her clothes, to meet her love did run,
In yonder vale lies cold and pale her constant farmer's son.

After spending a night and a day watching over her lover's body she returns home and accuses her two brothers.

Those villains confessed the murder, and for the same did
 die.
Young Mary she did fade away but never ceased to cry.
Her parents they did fade away. The glass of life had run.
Poor Mary sighed, and then she died for her constant
 farmer's son.

Of very much the same sort is the ballad of "Young Emily," or "Young Edmund," as it is variously entitled. Edmund is betrothed to Emily and then goes to sea to earn money for himself and his sweetheart. After seven years he returns loaded with gold which he triumphantly shows to Emily, and they plan that he shall lodge incognito at her father's public-house that night. But during the night

> Young Emily in her chamber
> She dreamt a dreadful dream.
> She dreamed she saw young Edmund
> Float in yon crystal stream.

She arises in the morning and questions her father, who confesses the murder of Edmund. Then she goes to the justice with her story, and her father is brought to trial.

> The jury found him guilty,
> And hanged he was also
> For the murder of young Edmund,
> Who plowed the Lowlands low.

Another Dream Ballad, composed on a motif that will be recognized by everyone who reads his Bible, is "The New York Trader." It differs from the conventional ballads of the class in that the dreamer is the criminal himself, and he reveals his guilt to a friend under the influence of the fear which has been imposed on him by the dream. This one is fairly brief, and I should like to quote it in full:

> To a New York trader I did belong.
> She was well built, both stout and strong.
> Well rigged, well manned, well fit for sea,
> Bound for New York in America.

> Our cruel captain, you do understand,
> Meant to starve us before we made the land.
> At length our hunger grew very great.
> We had but little on board to eat.

Being in necessity,
All by our captain's cruelty,
Our captain in the cabin lay;
He dreamt a dream, those words did say:

"Prepare yourselves and ship's company,
For tomorrow night you must lie with me."
Our captain awoke in a terrible fright,
It being the first watch of that night.

Loud for the bos'n he did call,
And to him related his secret all.
"Captain," said he, "if this be so,
O let none of your ship's crew know,
But keep your secrets in your breast,
And pray to God to give you rest."

"There is one thing more I have to tell.
When I in Waterford town did dwell
I killed my master, a merchant there,
All for the sake of his lady fair.

"I killed my wife and children three
All through that cursèd jealousy,
And on my servant laid the blame,
And hangèd he was for the same."

Early next morning a storm did rise,
Which caused the seamen much surprise.
The sea broke over us fore and aft
Till scarce a man on the deck was left.

Then the bos'n he did declare
Our captain was a murderer.
That so enraged all the ship's crew,
They overboard their captain threw.

When this was done a calm was there.
Our good light ship homeward did steer.
The wind abated and calmed the sea,
And we sailed safe to America.

And when we came to anchor there,
Our good light ship for to repair,
The people wondered much to see
What poor distressed shipwreck were we.

The Avenging Ghost motif operates in very much the same way. We have had illustrations of it in two of the ballads which I have had occasion to quote in earlier chapters, "The Greenwood Siding" and "The Gaspard Tragedy." In the former a mother murders her twin babies, and when she is returning home from her criminal expedition she meets the ghosts of "two babes a playing at ball"; in the latter William betrays and murders his sweetheart and goes to sea, but one night the ghost of his murdered Mary visits the ship, William is convicted of sin, "and raving distracted he died that same night." Another good illustration is an untitled ballad narrating the shadier side of the career of a Lothario-like sailor, who opens the ballad with a gay statement of his own life and habits, including the rather unctuous confession:

The female sex I did beguile,
And two of them I had with child.

One of these members of the "female sex" he marries, and the other he leaves to her fate, which is suicide. But Nemesis is on his track, and presently overtakes him.

One day as he was sailing on the mainmast high,
A little boat he chanced to spy,
And in that boat was a ghost so grim,
Which made him tremble in every limb.

It's to the deck this young man goes,
His mind to the captain for to disclose.
"O captain, captain, stand on my defense,
For here's a spirit coming hence."

It's on the deck the captain goes
To help this young man to face his foes.
"It is well known I was a maid
When first by you I was betrayed.

"You betrayed me once. I have you now.
I am a spirit come for you.
And now I've told you my mournful song,
All you who know where love belongs."

With great persuasions unto the boat
The young man he was forced to go.
The boat it sunk in a flame of fire,
Which made the ship's crew all admire.

I have dwelt long enough upon the "doleful matter" of
the various types of Murder Ballads, and must now turn
to another arbitrary and completely unrelated division.
Many of the later ballads, especially those of Irish origin,
are characterized by the introductory formula "Come all
you" or "Come all ye," and are classed generically as
"Come-all-ye's." Of these I have gathered a considerable
number in Nova Scotia. So far as motive or theme is concerned they show no sense of restriction, ranging the whole

gamut from stately themes of love and war down to the broad pleasantries of the music-hall song.

The formula of invitation is employed to specify the sort of audience that may be counted on to bring an intelligent and sympathetic appreciation to the narrative that follows. Sometimes this potential audience extends all-embracingly to the utmost limits of the world, as in the following inclusive invitation,

Come all you people, far and near.

In other cases a slight attempt at selection is made, as,

Come all ye men and maidens, and listen to my song.
If you pay good attention I'll not keep you long.

Or, as frequently happens, the doors are barred against all but the venerable:

Come all you aged people, I pray you lend an ear;
When you hear my feeling story you can't but shed a
    tear.

When a "Come-all-ye" celebrates an English victory the opening invitation is, naturally, addressed to those only who could be expected to feel a proper enthusiasm. The song of "The Battle of Alma" begins,

Come all you Britons, I pray give ear
To these few lines I've brought you here.

The geographical or racial line may be employed, also, merely to serve notice on the fellow-countrymen or neighbors of the hero in the action. The ballad of John Morrissey begins,

159

THE QUEST OF THE BALLAD

Come all you true Irish boys, please listen to me.
I will sing you the praises of John Morrissey.

The sea-ballads, when they open with an invitation, extend it, of course, to sea-faring men. The following are a few examples:

> Come all you jovial sailors bold,
>   The truth to you I write,
> Consarning of the raging sea
>   Which is my heart's delight.

Come all you jolly tarsmen, come listen to my song.
If you pay good attention I'll not keep you long.

Come all you bold seamen that plow the rough main.
Give ear to my story   The truth I'll explain.

The distinctions upon which the above invitations rest are all clear and consistent, but in other cases it is not so easy to understand the implied system of selection. Charles Augustus Andersen, for instance, makes the following subtle distinction in his choice of hearers:

Come all ye human countrymen, with pity lend an ear.

"Van Dieman's Land," which I have presented in an earlier chapter, is a ballad of the adventures and privations of three convicts, and yet it exhibits the most meticulous care in its selection of a "fit audience though few." It begins with the invitation,

Come all ye men of learning, and rambling boys beware.

and then proceeds to inculcate a proper frame of mind in the learned listeners:

It's when you go a hunting take your dog, your gun, your
    snare.
Think on lofty hills and mountains that are at your com-
    mand,
And think of the tedious journey going to Van Dieman's
    Land.

An equally snobbish point of view is adopted in the ballad of "Jack Donahue," which excludes from the circle of
listeners all but a narrow and highly specialized class:

Come all you gallant bushrangers and outlaws of disdain
Who scorn to dwell in slavery and wear the bonds of chains.
Attention pay to what I say and value it if you do.
I will relate the matchless fate of bold Jack Donahue.

The "Come-all-ye's" are almost infinite in number and
variety, but I have now discussed a sufficient number to
give some idea of the generic character indicated by the
designation which includes them all. And here, I think,
my rude attempt at a classification must end, since I have
discussed all the traits which are responsible for important
groupings in the ballads of my collection. It would be
possible, of course, to proceed with a series of narrower
groups, but many of the ballads here would have to be included also in some of the divisions already given. And
there would still remain a list of English and Scottish ballads on such a varied list of topics that to do them justice
I should have to discuss each of them in turn. The one
that I shall now cite, in order to drive home a last impression of the difficulty of categorizing, is only a trifle more
individual in its character than many others which I have
had to leave unrepresented.

O can you love little, O can you love long?
Can you love an old sweetheart till the new comes on?
Can you tell them you love them their minds for to ease?
And when their backs is turned to you, you can do as you
    please.

Yes, I can love little, I can love long.
I can love an old sweetheart till the new comes on.
I can tell them I love them their minds for to ease.
And when their backs is turned to me, I can do as I please.

As I was a walking one morning in spring
To hear the birds whistle and the nightingales sing
I saw a pretty fair maid. She's the one I adore.
I'll be her own true love on the New River Shore.

It's when my love's parents they came for to hear,
They pressed me away from my dearest dear.
They sent me away where loud cannons did roar,
And left her lamenting on the New River Shore.

It was three months after a letter she sent

.   .   .   .   .

Come back, my dearest Jimmie, you're the lad I adore,
And straight I'll go with you from the New River Shore.

I picked up my broadsword. It glittered all round.
A short time after laid seven to the ground.
Some bleeding, some dying, some wounded full sore,
I gained my own true love on the New River Shore.

O hard is the fate of all women kind.
They're always controlled, they're always confined.
Controlled by their parents until they're married wives,
Then slaves to their husbands all the rest of their lives.

In the opening stanzas of this versatile ballad we get the sinister suggestion that some forlorn maid is about to be left mourning the recreancy of her gay and faithless lover; and if this were the case we could place it, along with "the Butcher Boy," and a few others, under some such heading as Ballads of Forsaken Maids. But next we proceed to the forced separation of two lovers and then to their happy reunion at the apparently trifling expense of a few slain and wounded comrades—or enemies. This furnishes nothing more definite than the heading, Separation and Reunion of Lovers. And finally we take leave of the situation, whatever it may be, with a last haunting reflection upon the miseries of oppressed maidens, and with the added bitterness of discovering that their state is not relieved even by marriage.

This superadded motive in the last line is the one which, at least, characterized the ballad in the opinion of the person who aided me in preserving it. I had been engaged for hours in coaxing one ballad after another from an ancient and obstinate lady who insisted that in spite of my apparent honesty I was preparing to have a vast deal of fun at her expense, and who stoutly averred, moreover, that she did not know any ballads now, no matter what might be proved concerning her past life. At the close of one of her recitations, when she settled back with the usual declaration that she had come to the end of her tether at last, her daughter good-naturedly came to my aid. The latter, a fine buxom matron, repeated the last stanza of "The New River Shore," and bade her mother "go ahead with that," at the same time observing, as she folded her muscular arms and looked benignly upon her small and palpably uxorious husband in the chimney-corner, "Ye

163

may depend I'll never forget that verse. I've got blame good reasons for rememberin' that to me sorrow." In the absence, then, of any undisputed evidence in favor of either of the captions given above we might as well fall in with the suggestion of my jocular friend, who, if she had been a pedantic person with classifying tendencies, would have placed "The New River Shore" under the caption, Ballads of Oppressed Wives.

CHAPTER EIGHT

The Inconstancy of the Ballad

One winter night, some years ago, I was disporting myself in base fashion at a country dance in a remote region of northern Nova Scotia. The pauses between dances were being utilized by hot-headed youths in settling their various disputes and rivalries, and by their more pacific seniors in spinning yarns around the kitchen stove; and towards the end of the composite entertainment an old fisherman led a plangent chorus of voices through the "Come-all-ye" ballad of "The Plains of Waterloo":

> Come all you brisk and lively lads,
>   Come listen unto me,
> While I relate how I have fought
>   Through the wars of Germany.
>
> I have fought through Spain and Portugal,
>   Through France and Flanders too,—

Up to this point the different members of the roaring crew all agreed in the one constant recollection of their campaigning days, but now they suddenly broke into two divisions on a rather important autobiographical detail. One group sang the remaining two lines of the second stanza,

> But it's little I thought I'd be reserved
>   For the plains of Waterloo.

The veterans of the other group, with a less cheerful recollection of their experiences on the great battle-field, sang with a loud and mournful insistence,

> But it's little I thought it would be my fate
> For to die on Waterloo.

There was an immediate halt followed by a savage argument, but, so far as I can remember, not one of the contestants attempted to settle the case on its own merits. Every man contended that he had sung the verse "the way it ought to be sung," and many of them appealed to authority and tradition; but if I in my wisdom had suggested that a man would not be likely to make a song about the Battle of Waterloo if he had been killed in that battle I should undoubtedly have been assured with profane laconicism, "It don't make a damn' bit of difference about that. We're singin' the song the way it was made."

There you have, in little, the attitude of ballad-singers the world over. I think it is safe to say that no true ballad-singer ever consciously changed a line or even a word in the songs which he received from his fathers and passed on to his children; but everyone who has the slightest acquaintance with ballads knows that they exhibit the most startling variations in phraseology, so that even within the limits of a single community a given stanza may be sung in several different ways. In this brief chapter I shall illustrate a few of the characteristic variations and idiosyncrasies in the ballads that have been sung to me.

In another chapter I have told the story of my gradual acquisition of the old ballad of "Little Musgrave." The title itself had been metamorphosed into "Little Matha Grove" somewhere in that misty land where ballads change

166

their form when no eye is upon them. One singer told me that in his opinion the name of the protagonist was "Little Matey Groney," and if he had been a singer of note and an authority in the places where ballads were sung he might quite conceivably have imposed his vaguely imagined substitution upon a large circle of singers and thus have handed it on to posterity. The other singers of the ballad, however, all employed what we may now regard as the conservative name "Little Matha Grove." But in designating the husband whose position was for a brief season usurped by Little Matha with such tragic consequences there was a more important and mystifying difference. In Child's editions of the ballad the husband is Lord Bernard or Lord Barnett, but in some of the versions that I have collected he is called Lord Daniel and in others he is called Lord Arnold. All of the versions that I have found were within a radius of five or six miles, and in no case was the singer able to offer any argument except that Lord Daniel—or Lord Arnold—was the right name because it was the one used when the song was sung to him; and if we could follow the ballad back through the long centuries that have elapsed since its inception, questioning the different singers along the way, we should doubtless receive from every singer the same reason for the faith that was in him respecting every variant name and phrase that he employed.

But in the phrasing of several lines and stanzas of "Little Matha Grove" there are variations for which we may account easily enough in our learned fashion, though our explanations would seem to the singers quite foolish and beside the point.

Little Matha and Lord Daniel's—or Lord Arnold's—

167

wife are thus described by one singer in their brief hour of felicity:

So they tossed and tumbled all that night.

and by another singer thus:

So they hustled and they tumbled till they both fell asleep.

In describing an incident of this sort any singer, under the influence of embarrassment or of unctuosity, as the case may be, will unconsciously employ the euphemisms that he is most accustomed to. And even easier to explain is the variation in the injured husband's response to Little Matha's protest that he is unprepared to fight for his life against an antagonist who has "two bright swords by his side." In one version the answer is:

> If I have two bright swords by my side
>   They cost me deep in purse,
> And you shall have the best of them,
>   And I shall have the worst.
>
> And you shall have the very first blow,
>   And I shall have the other.
> What more, then, could I do for you
>   If you were my own born brother?

and in another the two stanzas are fused into one in the following wise:

> You shall have the very best one,
>   And I shall have the worst,
> And you shall have the very first blow,
>   And I shall have the next.

This fusion is probably the result of a defective recollection of the complete answer combined with a very clear recollection of the gist of the answer, which results in an unconscious bringing together of the main points in the chivalrous response of the husband.

I have hunted down five different persons who were able to sing this noble old ballad in some fashion, and the five versions are teeming with variations of this sort, more or less capable of explanation. It is interesting, then, to see the unanimity of all these versions in retaining an earlier variation which had the effect of completely ruining the rhyme of the stanza in which it appeared. This stanza occurs about the beginning of the ballad, and describes the appearance of the richly-arrayed persons who were coming to church "the holy word to hear." In the older version of the ballad which appears in Child's collection the stanza runs thus:

> The one of them was clad in green,
>> Another was clad in pall,
> And then came in my Lord Bernard's wife,
>> The fairest amongst them all.

and in all the versions that I have heard the stanza takes this form:

> Some came in in diamonds of gold,
>> And some came in in pearls,
> And among them all was little Matha Grove,
>> The handsomest of them all.

The interesting change, of course, is from "pall" to "pearls." The "diamonds of gold" would come in naturally enough to accompany the pearls and to supplant the green, and the substitution of Little Matha Grove for Lord Bernard's wife is only one of scores of examples of fast-and-loose playing with proper names in the ballads. But the change from "pall" to "pearls" is the change from an unknown to a known word—a purchase of reason at a ruinous expense of rhyme. Lacking the omniscience to report exactly how the change came about, one may shrewdly surmise that it was never definitely or consciously made, but that, in an age that knew not "pall" except as a sombre burden to be borne decorously to the grave, the more richly suggestive "pearls" came creeping in during the night to find themselves securely established in the morning and ready to proceed to church on their hypo-critical mission "the holy word to hear."

An equally heroic sacrifice of rhyme in the cause of reason appears in the modern version of "Lord Thomas and Fair Ellinor" as I found it in Nova Scotia. Everybody who knows the tragic tale in the old ballad will remember how the "brown girl," when she is eclipsed at her own wedding by her beautiful rival Fair Ellinor, draws her "little penknife" and stabs Ellinor to the heart. In the old version in Child's collection Ellinor is thus addressed by Lord Thomas after she has received her death wound:

"Oh Christ now save thee," Lord Thomas he said,
  "Methinks thou look'st wondrous wan;
Thou wast used for to look with as fresh a colour
  As ever the sun shin'd on."

and in the Nova Scotia version the stanza runs:

The Inconstancy of the Ballad

"Oh what is the matter?"   Lord Thomas he said,
  "I think you look wonderful pale;
You used to have as bright a colour
  As ever the sun shone on."

Another demonstration of the fact that the word "wan" has ceased to be a popular descriptive epithet appears in my Nova Scotia version of "The Douglas Tragedy." Lord William has slain, one by one, the seven brethren and the father of Lady Margret.   Then the two lovers proceed on their elopement, or, as the old version in Child narrates it,

O they rode on, and on they rode,
  And a' by the light of the moon,
Until they came to yon wan water,
  And there they lighted down.

This stanza is thus varied in the Nova Scotia version:

'Twas on the road, 'twas away they rode,
  'Twas all by the light of the moon,
Until they came to the Erint waters,
  That was raging like the main.[1]

---

[1] In the Scotch ballad "May Collin" (Version H of "Lady Isabel and the Elf Knight" in Child's collection) the following stanza narrates the journey of May and her false lover to the river-side:

They had not ridden a mile, a mile,
  A mile but barely three,
Till they came to a rank river,
  Was raging like the sea.

This stanza, to be sure, does not appear in the versions of the ballad which I have found in Nova Scotia, under the title "Pretty Polly." It did appear, however, in some older versions in Scotland, and, very probably, in some of the Nova Scotia versions as well; and one may conjecture that, either in Scotland or in Nova Scotia, it influenced "The Seven Brethren" to the extent of bringing about the variation in the fourth line of this stanza.

"The Douglas Tragedy," or "The Seven Brethren" as it is called in Nova Scotia, was sung to me by Bob Langille of Tatamagouche. When we reached this stanza in the course of the hand-paralyzing process of copying out the ballad I paused to light my pipe, Bob thankfully followed suit, and in the millennial atmosphere of peace created by the synchronous action of two pipes I asked Bob what the Erint waters might be. "Why," said Bob, "that's the name of the river, and it would be one of them great rivers in England, of course. I never seen it me-self, but if ye look in yer jography ye'll most likely find out all about it." Bob is the only person that ever sang "The Douglas Tragedy" for me, and whether he was the one to transmute "wan" to "Erint" I cannot say, but I have made it evident that he never, at least, performed any conscious act of transmutation, nor, one may pretty safely say, was any such act ever performed by any singer to bring about the change.

These last three examples would seem to indicate the existence of two principles operative in ballads which are being moulded by the process of oral transmission, name-ly, that unfamiliar words are replaced by familiar ones and that rhyme is not an important consideration as com-pared with reason. But if I were to accept these as rules and then proceed in a spirit of honesty to illustrate them from the popular ballads I should be compelled to spend fully half of my time in chronicling the exceptions, of which I shall now give two or three examples.

The last stanza of the ballad of "Van Dieman's Land," as it was sung to me by old James Langille of Marshville, runs as follows:

O last night as I lay upon my bed I had a pleasant dream;
I dreamt I was in old Ireland down by a spurling stream,
With a handsome girl upon my side and she at my com-
    mand,
When I woke quite broken-hearted all in Van Dieman's
    Land.

"Purling," it need scarcely be said, is to the popular in-
telligence unmeaning and unfamiliar. But, aided by the
initial sibilant, it grows rich in onomatopeic suggestion.
It may be objected that "spurling" was quite possibly
James's individual improvement on the original word, but
I have been told by persons who heard the song in the old
days, before the ballads grew mortally ill, that "spurling"
is traditional in that region. At any rate, James had
not the slightest idea what the word was, but he nevertheless dwelt upon it with special emphasis and unction when
he sang the song to me, and if he had just then come from
a reading of Keats he would undoubtedly have silenced my
criticisms, if I had made them, with the retort:

Beauty is truth, truth beauty,—that is all
Ye know on earth, and all ye need to know.

A variation of a slightly different character occurs in
the first stanza of the slashing sea-ballad of "Kelly the
Pirate," which was sung to me by that ancient mariner,
Dick Hinds. The stanza, as it was rendered with sonorous melody by Dick, runs thus:

Captain Cooper gave orders on the first of May
To cruise in the Channel for our enemy,
To protect our commerce from that darren foe,
And all our merchant ships where they would go.

"Darren" is obviously a corruption of "daring," but it must not be interpreted as a mere mispronunciation of the latter word. No one who had ever heard Dick sing the ballad could think of offering that explanation. If the word were written "dahrren" it would more truly represent the actual pronunciation, and it is pronounced with a savage and powerful trilling of the r. The change may have been wrought upon the word in the innumerable fo'c'stles where it was absorbed and reanimated by Dick, or it may have been made instinctively and naturally by Dick himself, to whom sound and fury were dear; but whatever the explanation it cannot be denied that a rational but colorless word has been transformed into an irrational epithet of richly blasphemous and opprobrious connotation, the sort of epithet that any one of us might gladly employ when we speak of our enemies.

Another example of the irrational and meaningless word unquestioningly retained in the belief that it is correct, even though unintelligible, occurs in one of my versions of "Pretty Polly," which is the modern substitute for the old title "Lady Isabel and the Elf Knight." When Polly returns from the river where she has drowned her false lover the parrot from its cage asks an excited question which awakens Polly's father and comes near to giving away the whole escapade. But when the father inquires the cause of the parrot's excitement the latter, with ready wit, shields its mistress with the following reply:

The old cat had got up to my littock so high,
    And I was afraid she was going to eat me,
And I was calling for Pretty Polly
    To go drive the old cat away.

This stanza occurs in the version sung to me by Easter Ann Langille, daughter of George Langille of Marshville, one of the old heroic race of ballad singers who was gathered to his fathers in consequence of my determination to seek him out and copy down all the ballads that he knew— all of which I have related in a previous chapter of this book. When Easter Ann had finished singing the ballad to me I asked her what a littock was, and she regarded me for a space with a sardonic eye.

"Well now," she said at last, "I know what ye'll be askin' me for next. Ye'll be askin' me to write a dictionary for ye to take back to College with ye. If a great scholar like you doesn't know what a littock is, I'd like to know how ye can expect a poor ignorant old woman to know."

I should have liked to ask a similar question of old Ann Thompson regarding an astounding line in one of her ballads, but the reader who remembers my encounter with Ann in the first chapter of this book will not think too meanly of me when I say that I copied the line down with never a flicker of an eyelid, accepting it as though it were the most glorified commonsense or the simplest and clearest of narrative details. The ballad in question was "The Banks of Claudie," which began quietly and modestly enough with the stanza:

As I walked out one evening down by the river side
I overheard a damsel, the tears fell from her eyes,
Saying, "This is a dark and stormy night,"—those very
  words did say—
"And my love is on the raging sea bound for America."

The "I," it will at once be obvious, is the returned lover in disguise, and he proceeds after the manner of his type in the ballads to test the faithfulness of his mourning sweetheart with such insinuating remarks as, "Do not trust young Johnny, for he's a false young man," and "Come along with me to yonder banks, no danger need you fear." Angered by this persecution, the young woman pronounces upon her supposedly absent lover a eulogistic stanza in which the fervor is perhaps a sufficient reason for the remarkable statement in the last line. This is the stanza:

If Johnny he was here this night he'd shed me from all
    harm;
He's dressed in his readiness all in his uniform.
He's gone to plow the ocean, his foes he will defy.
Like a rolling king of honour he fought in the wars of
    Troy.

Ann delivered this stanza with her black defiant eyes fixed steadily upon me, and even that Homeric warrior Johnny, if he had been in my place, would have hesitated to insinuate that anything in the song might be obscure or queer.

I might go on with numberless exceptions to the perilous rule that humble folk like to understand the expressions that occur in their songs, but if I have conveyed the impression that in this case the exceptions proceed *pari passu* with the rule I may now go on to examine the second principle which I sceptically proposed a few pages back, namely, that rhyme is in itself a restriction to be swept aside when it stands in the way of satisfactory expression. Let me present one or two exceptions to this experimental dictum.

The reader may remember that in one of the earlier chapters of this book I discussed a group of ballads presenting the story of the young man who has returned to his home after several years' absence, and who, under cover of a disguise, proceeds to test the fidelity of his former sweetheart. The ballad which I cited as an example of this class begins with the stanza:

> As a maid was walking in her garden
>   A single sailor came riding by;
> He stepped up to her, he thought he knew her,
>   He said, "Fair maid, can you fancy I?"

If, after a due contemplation of this stanza, anyone still feels inclined to maintain that the ballad-singing folk are careless and neglectful of rhyme when it stands in the way of rational expression, I have only one further expedient to employ, which is to refer him to a stanza occurring about midway in the rollicking English ballad of "The Liverpool Landlady." Sailor John has just returned from sea with his pockets full of gold, and he proceeds to call upon his former landlady and to make trial of her altruism by pretending that he is penniless. The landlady fails miserably to conform to the ethical standards of John, and at last he punishes her horribly by diving into his pockets and producing "his two hands full of gold." The landlady's consternation is thus depicted:

> The sight of the money made the old woman rave,
> To see that the sailor had plenty for to gave.
> "While you were in earnest, John, I am only in jest,
> Of all my old boarders, John, I like you the best."

177

Here is rhyme with a vengeance. In the enthusiasm aroused by this example and the one cited just before it I am almost tempted to proceed to the unscientific generalization that ballad-singers will gladly sacrifice upon the altar of rhyme all of those considerations which ordinarily operate in speech, heaping up grammar, idiom, reason, and coherence in one indiscriminate oblation. I am restrained from this perilous decision, however, by the remembrance that these two examples were presented as exceptions to a rule tentatively established on what seemed for the moment to be a tolerably firm basis of illustration, and I shall content myself, therefore, with a reiteration of the conservative principle that no rule for variant phrasing in the popular ballads is stronger than its exceptions.

But no reader, I hope, will be so unwary as to suppose that I am gradually working myself into a state of despair by a contemplation of the infinite variety of the popular ballads. There needs no Daniel to come to judgment to tell us that infinite variety and elusiveness are alluring things in a woman, and these same things form an equally considerable part of the fascination of the popular ballads. Furthermore, so long as any ballad remains popular, these qualities cling to it as a matter of course. I may copy down and commit to cold print the version of a ballad which is given to me by a singer of the people, but I must on no account permit myself to suppose that this version represents anything like a rigid or final form of the ballad in question. No version of any ballad has the right to be considered as either rigid or final. It is of the very essential nature of all ballads that, so long as they remain popular, they are capable of Protean variations in phraseology, and the only standard of etiquette to apply is that these variations must be instinctive and unconscious. Bishop Percy and the other collectors of his school who deliberately tampered with the phraseology of the ballads which they were committing to print were infringing upon a rule which to every singer of the folk is sacred and inviolable.

The ballad collectors of the old school had little hesitation about "improving" and "polishing" the phraseology of any ballad which they had found and were about to commit to print, and nowadays every puny whipster is ready to castigate their shadows for this sacrilege. The old collectors, as a matter of fact, were guilty only of a failure to appreciate the true nature and worth of folklore, and in our own days of enlightenment we are guilty of a misapprehension almost equally great. I myself have heard collectors speak of one special version of a ballad as being "the correct version" and of other versions equally popular as being "incorrect"; and a fairly common method with conscientious collectors is to persuade a singer to go over a ballad again and again until finally the so-called "correct" form is beaten out. This, to be sure, is an interesting experiment to perform both with the singer and with the ballad, if the singer is an amenable person, which is not invariably the case; but the scientific purpose of the experiment should be to discover how many variations this particular singer will employ in singing this particular ballad, and not to arrive at a falsely hypothesized "correct" form. Here, for instance, are two slightly varied forms of a stanza from "Lord Thomas and Fair Ellinor." They appeared, respectively, in the first and second renditions of the ballad from one singer.

> He took her by the lily-white hand
> And led her through the hall,
> He set her on a golden chair
> Among the ladies all.

and,

> He took her by the lily-white hand
> And led her through them all,
> He set her on a golden chair
> Among the ladies all.

Two stanzas before this one occurs the description of Fair Ellinor as she went with her merry maids to the ill-fated wedding of Lord Thomas. The singer to whom I have just alluded is Lucy Langille of Marshville, and she thus worded the description when she first sang the ballad to me:

> She dressed herself in riches so gay,
> Her merry maids all in blue,
> And every town that she passed through
> They took her to be a queen.

As I was copying the stanza down I asked rather ill-advisedly, "Are you sure she dressed them in blue and not in green?" "Yes," said Lucy, " 'blue' is right. Ye can see it rhymes with 'through.' " I made no further objection, but when I persuaded her to sing the ballad for me a second time, she delivered the stanza, without any hesitation, thus:

> She dressed herself in riches so gay,
> Her merry maids all in green,
> And every town that she passed by
> They took her to be a queen.

The one thing that I felt positive of at the time was that there was no deliberate change made, but since I played a part in bringing this particular change about I can not, as an honest collector, use it without explanation in any version of the ballad which I present. The variation is in its way, however, an interesting and characteristic one. It has an exact parallel in the two variants of a stanza in "Lord Bateman." This ballad, it may be remembered, was sung to me, on two different occasions, by Sandy and Dave Rogers respectively, and they had both learned it in bygone days from their common father. Sandy thus portrayed the prompt action of Lord Bateman upon receipt of the tidings that his Turkish lady has arrived at the palace:

> He stamped his foot all on the floor,
>   He broke the table in pieces four,
> Saying, "Adieu, adieu to my new wedded bride,
>   For this fair maid I'll go and see."

while Dave reported the action thus:

> He stamped his foot upon the floor,
>   He broke the table in pieces three,
> Saying, "Adieu, adieu to my new wedded bride,
>   For this fair lady I'll go and see."

In this case, of course, one has a perfect right to prefer Dave's stanza to Sandy's, since the latter is obviously a corruption caused by Sandy's instinctive eagerness in reaching for the immediate rhyme instead of waiting calmly for the ultimate one which is in harmony with the neighboring stanzas; and the same principle of selection could be applied to my preceding example from "Lord Thomas and Fair Ellinor" if my own artificial influence had not helped to produce the variation.

But one rarely has the opportunity to be as definite as this in comparing variant words or phrases. Mutations are likely to appear in a ballad during the process of repeated singing by one person, they are certain to appear in great variety and profusion in a ballad that is the common property of several persons, and to select from this interesting confusion one form which shall be labelled "correct" is to remove from the term "ballad" its qualifying epithet "popular." The singers themselves are always extremely anxious to be correct, and every variation which they unconsciously introduce is of importance if one is to accept the ballad as a "popular" possession.

I have shown something of the nature of this confusion as it appears in many of the ballads that I have mentioned in this chapter, but I should like to examine some one ballad rather more consistently from this point of view. The most extreme example that I could select from my own collection would be "Little Musgrave," or "Little Matha Grove." This was sung to me by five different persons, and each of the five consequent versions has its own striking peculiarities. But a fairer illustration, and one that will be easier to present, is "Lady Isabel and the Elf Knight," or "Pretty Polly," as it is more simply entitled in Nova Scotia when it is given a title at all in that region. "Pretty Polly" was sung to me by John Langille of River John and by Easter Ann Langille of Marshville; and Dave Rogers of Pictou, though he could not remember the ballad well enough to sing it throughout, was nevertheless able to give me what he regarded as the "correct" versions of two or three stanzas. Some of the variations which thus appeared I shall now exhibit.

John started the ballad with these four stanzas:

> There was a lord in Ambertown,
>   He courted a lady gay,
> And all that he wanted of this pretty maid
>   Was to take her life away.
>
> Go get me some of your father's gold,
>   And some of your mother's fee,
> And two of the best nags out of the stable,
>   Where there stands thirty and three.
>
> She went and got some of her father's gold,
>   And some of her mother's fee,
> And two of the best nags out of the stable,
>   Where there stood thirty and three.
>
> She mounted on the milk-white steed,
>   And he on the rambling gray,
> And they rode till they came to the salt sea-side,
>   Three hours before it was day.

Easter Ann condensed these four stanzas to three in the following wise:

> There was a lord in Ambertown
>   Courted a lady fair,
> And all he wanted of this pretty fair maid
>   Was to take her life away.

Go get me some of your father's gold,
   And some of your mother's fees,
And two of the best horses in your father's stall
   Where there stands thirty and three.

So she mounted on her steed white milk,
   And he on his dappling gray,
And they rode forward to the sea
   Two hours before it was day.

So far these two singers have not agreed entirely on more than two or three lines, and some of the differences, like the rationalized form "fees" in Easter Ann's version as against the conservative form "fee" retained by John, are not without interest. John was content with the word "fee" because, although he had no idea what it meant, he was convinced that it was right. Easter Ann, out of many unhappy experiences, knew full well what "fees" were, and how fortunate was the maid who could collect and retain them.

The ballad now proceeds to the point where the villainous wooer commands his victim to remove her rich clothing before she goes to join the six other maids whom he has "drownded here." In John's version the order is given in this form:

   "Take off, take off thy silken dress,
      Likewise thy golden stays.
   Methinks they are too rich and too gay
      To rot in the salt salt seas."

Easter Ann varied the first line of this stanza with

   "Take off, take off thy bonny silk plaid."

The lady prepares to obey this request, but, with a wily assumption of modesty, requests her companion to turn his back while she undresses. The moment he does so she seizes him "by the middle so tight" and throws him into the water to keep company with the six pretty maids whom he has previously drowned. Then she mounts her horse, rides back home "an hour before it was day," and prepares to enter the house quietly when she is interrupted by the parrot, which is training a keen weather eye upon her actions. John's version thus introduces the parrot:

> The parrot being up so early in the morn,
>   It unto Polly did say,
> "I was afraid that some ruffian
>   Had led you astray."

Easter Ann's version agrees; but at this point Dave comes in with an interesting variation, which is

> The parrot was up in the window high
>   And heard what she did say.
> "Where have you been, my pretty Polly,
>   That you're out so long before day?"

The following stanza, in John's version, runs,

> The old man on his pillow did lie,
>   He unto the parrot did say,
> "What ails you, what ails you, you pretty
>   Poll parrot,
>   You prattle so long before day?"

and in Easter Ann's version it assumes the following strange and vertiginous aspect:

The old man he, its being awoke,
And he heard all that was said.
"What were you prittling and prattling, my
pretty Polly,
And keeping me awake all night long?"

The parrot, in spite of the frightful manhandling which
he thus receives, recovers his wits immediately, and sallies
to the rescue of his mistress with the explanation,

"The old cat had got up to my littock so high,
And I was afraid she was going to eat me.
And I was calling for pretty Polly
To go drive the old cat away."

John's version of this stanza differs in the first line, and
ennobles the cat with the masculine gender. It runs,

"The old cat was at my cage door,
And I was afraid he was going to eat me,
And I was calling for pretty Polly
To go drive the old cat away."

But here Dave comes in again, this time with a startling
variation:

"The old cat was at my cage door,
And swore she would devour me,
And I was calling for fair MacConnel
To hiss the cat away."

After Dave had sung this outrageous stanza to me I
told him how John and Easter Ann had sung it, and de-

manded an explanation. "Why," said Dave complacent-
ly, "it's plain to be seen that I sung the verse right for ye.
Fair MacConnel was the servant-girl's name, and neither
one o' *them* could remember it for ye, could they?"

This brings us to the conclusion of the ballad, which con-
tains a grateful recognition from the lady of the service
rendered her by the parrot. John's version closes with
the two graceful and flowing stanzas,

> "Well turned, well turned, my pretty Poll parrot!
> "Well turned, well turned!" said she.
> "Your cage it shall be of the glittering gold,
> And the doors of ivory.
>
> "No tales, no tales, my pretty Poll parrot,
> No tales you will tell on me.
> Your cage it shall be of the glittering gold,
> And hung on yon willow tree."

But John himself was impressed not so much by the beauty
of the verses as by the incomprehensible nature, as it
seemed to him, of the last promise. "I can't rightly see,"
he objected, "what good it would do the parrot to have
he's cage taken away out there. That always seemed to
me to be a hell of a distance away from the house to put
a bird-cage."

The source of John's perplexity will be more evident if
I present a stanza which occurs earlier in the ballad:

> "If I take off my silken dress,
> Likewise my golden stays,
> You must turn your back around to me,
> And face yon willow tree."

That is to say, "yon willow tree" was by the "salt sea-side," two hours' journey from the house.

But Easter Ann had no such problem in higher criticism to knot her brows. The concluding stanza of her version comfortably evades the issue with a very interesting line, which is the last line of the ballad, and, solely for that reason, the last variant to be found.

"Don't prittle, don't prattle, my pretty Polly,
  Nor tell any tales on me.
Your cage shall be made of the glittering gold
  Instead of the greenwood tree."

I might go on almost indefinitely heaping up similar examples of popular variations in the renditions of the ballads, but I have now suggested most of the characteristic kinds of change in the ballads that I myself have heard. My interest in doing so, I need hardly say, is in pointing out something of the endless variety displayed by the ballad when it is the possession of its natural owners, the humble folk, and I have religiously kept myself from drifting into the formulation of any rigid theory of change. It would be more proper, I suppose, to say that I have been kept from any such theorizing by the ballads themselves, since they steadily refuse to lend themselves to any rule formulated either by an individual or by a group of persons, preferring the freedom which permits them to change according to the chance mood dictated by time, place, or singer. I have, to be sure, insisted in rather didactic fashion on the good faith of the singers who are the instruments for producing the changes, but I can do no less after my scores of experiences in the company of singers who, with never a dissenting voice, have combined to nourish this belief in me.

In so far, then, as this chapter has veered towards the uncharted rocks of theory it has been steered by the sing-ers and not by the ballads. I have laid constant stress on my belief that no ballad-singer ever makes a conscious or deliberate change in the phraseology of his song, and so far, at least, as my own experience goes, there is not a shred of evidence against this belief. If one were to con-sider the whole question of ballad change one could not, of course, be content with a consideration of the influence of the folk singers only. It would be necessary to admit certain other known influences, and to guess at still others which are uncertain and unknown. The fact, for instance, that a version of a traditional ballad was often captured and printed in a song-book or in broadside form with "corrections" and "improvements," and then circulated afresh among people to whom the authority of the printed word was absolute, is one that would have to be definitely considered. But with such influences as these I have at present no concern. I am accepting the many and puz-zling variations as they occur, and attempting only to show, on a basis of illustration, the attitude of the singers as I have found them.

A truce, then, to theorizing. An expedient that occurs to me as a useful one to aid in fixing a complete and haunt-ing conviction of the variableness of the ballad which has been allowed to go untrammelled among the singers of the folk is to present in full, with all their picturesque differ-ences, the two versions that I have collected of a modern metrical tale which in its time has been dear to many a sailor's heart. This is the ballad that I have already re-ferred to as "The Liverpool Landlady." I first heard it,

under the title "Green Beds," from old Bob Langille, and
he had learned it in the days of his comparative youth
down at the wharf in Tatamagouche, where he used to find
an occasional day's work at the unloading of the schooners.   His version proceeded in this wise:

'Twas of a young sailor
    Who's lately come ashore,
He's ragged in his apparel
    Like one that is poor.

He came unto the boarding-house
    That he used to board in.
He came unto the old woman
    To see what she would say to him.

"You're welcome home, dear Johnnie,
    You're welcome home from sea.
Last night my daughter Mollie
    Was dreaming of thee.

"What news, what news, dear Johnnie?
    What news you brought from sea?"
"Bad news, bad news," says Johnnie,
    For all is gone from me.

"The ship has sprung a leaking,
    And all is gone from me,
And the last of my money
    Is drownded in the sea.

"Call down your daughter Mollie,
    Call her down to me,
And we'll drink and drown our sorrow
    And married we shall be."

THE INCONSTANCY OF THE BALLAD

"My daughter she is busy,
　Nor can she come to you.
Neither will I trust you
　With one bowl or two."

When Johnnie heard this
　He hung down his head,
And called for a candle
　To light himself to bed.

"The green beds are full, John,
　And have been for a week.
So for some other lodgings
　You must go for to seek."

When Johnnie heard this,
　He hung down his head,
And called for his reckoning
　Which he had to pay.

"You owe me thirty shillings, John,
　With something of the old."
With that he pulled out
　His two hands full of gold.

When the old woman saw this
　She began to rue,
Saying, "For the future, Johnnie,
　I'm not quite done of you.

"If you had been in earnest, John,
　As I was in a jest,
By my reputation, Johnnie,
　I love you the best.

"The green beds are empty, John,
  And have been all the week,
For you and my daughter
  To take a pleasant sleep."

"I won't lie in your green beds,
  I'd rather lie in the street.
For when I was in poverty,
  Lodgings was for to seek.

"But now that I've got plenty
  I'll walk the streets alone,
With my brown jug and quart mug,
  And tumblers in galore."

About a year after I had copied this ballad out and committed it to imperishable manuscript I was spending a comfortable evening with Dick Hinds. After we had employed a fruitful hour or two in ferreting out the hidden places in Canadian politics Dick suddenly straightened up in his chair, spat violently into the glowing embers of his kitchen fire, and exclaimed: "Well, it's about time I was singin' ye a song. I'll give ye 'The Liverpool Landlady' this time fer a change."

No assent or encouragement was expected from me. I merely separated a sulphur match from the card on the little shelf behind the stove and put the tip of it against a red-hot area to get a fresh flame for my pipe, while Dick cleared his throat gigantically, threw his head back to get more sea-room, and directed towards the ceiling the resonant strains of the following song:

The Inconstancy of the Ballad

I'll tell you a story, I'll not keep you long,
Concerning a sailor whose name it was John.
He had made a gallant voyage to sea and just returned to
  shore,
He was ragged and dirty as though he was poor.

He went to the house where he used to lodge in,
He called for a glass of the very best gin.
"You're welcome home, dear Johnny, you're welcome
  home from sea,
Last night my daughter Polly was dreaming of thee.

"She dreamed that you made a successful voyage,
She dreamed that you brought home a lot of foreign toys."
O, John he sighed and said, "My voyage it has been
  crossed,
Upon the wide ocean our ship and cargo lost.

Call down your daughter Polly and set her down by me,
And fetch in some liquor for us to have a spree."
"My daughter Polly is busy, John, nor shall she come to
  thee,
Nor neither will I trust you for a glass, two, or three."

O, John he being drowsy he hung down his head,
He asked for a candle to light him to bed.
"My beds are all full, John, and has been all the week,
Therefore some other lodgings you must go and seek."

"How much do I owe you?" the sailor then he said.
"Come, make out your bill, and down it shall be paid."
"Five and forty shillings, John, you owed to me of old."
With that he pulled out his two hands full of gold.

The sight of the money made the old woman rave,
To see that the sailor had plenty for to gave.
"While you were in earnest, John, I am only in jest.
Of all my old boarders, John, I like you the best.

"I'll call down my daughter Polly and set her on your
knee.
I'll bring in plenty liquor for you to have a spree.
The green bed is empty, John, and has been all last week,
Where you and my daughter Polly can take a silent sleep."

"Before I'd lie in your house I'd lie into my grave.
You thought I had no money. On me you played the
knave.
It's when a man's got money, he can rant and roar,
With brown jugs and quart mugs and tumblers in galore."

Come all you bold sailors that ploughs the rough main,
That do earn your money in cold winds and rain,
When you do get it, pray lay it up in store.
Without that companion you're turned out of door.

This was palpably a version of the same song that Bob
had sung to me a year before, although the title was new,
the phraseology differed as one man's account of an incident will differ from another man's, and the tune was arranged so as to bring two of Bob's short-line verses into
the surf-like roll of a single long-metre stanza. I did not
diminish Dick's triumph in the performance by telling him
that I had heard the song before, but only asked him where
he had learned it. "Ho! God bless me, how do I know
where I larned it?" roared Dick. "I s'pose it would be in
the fo'c'stle, when I was restin' up after doin' me turn at
the wheel, but I don't know. How kin ye expect a man to

know where he larnt a song that he's ben singin' all he's life?"

Dick's virile response to my pedantic inquiry seems to me, on mature consideration, to be filled with a rich and powerful suggestiveness. If it had come to my mind before I began this chapter I might have been spared the necessity of much solemn reasoning about the wherefore and the why of lines and phrases which have grown up in the ballads as vernal twigs appear upon the thriving tree, and the reader would have profited by my abstention. But even a belated wisdom is better than a continuance in folly, and to all the fruitless inquiries concerning ballad variants which press upon me for further consideration in this chapter I shall now oppose the steadfast reply, "God bless me, how do I know where they came from?"

CHAPTER NINE

NATIVE SONGS AND TRADITIONS

In a country so resonant with English and Scotch ballads as Nova Scotia was fifty years ago it would have been a strange thing if some native bards had not been inspired to produce poetic narrative of the traditional sort. As a matter of fact the local bard seems to have been in those days a rather familiar figure, and by a rare accident one may still find traces of his footprints in the sand—pious or lugubrious fragments of song composed in honor of a murder, a shipwreck, or some such notable event. Ballad-making is in a perilous state when it is vivified only by the shock of a sudden horror or catastrophe, but it has never enjoyed, so far as I can find, a much greater security in Nova Scotia—any more than it has, for that matter, in the parent country itself during the recent period which covers the settlement of Nova Scotia.

On the two insistent topics of murder and shipwreck, however, many an inglorious Milton has been moved to descant. The consequent ballads in most cases enjoyed a brief popularity in the districts where the events themselves were cause for excitement, and then perished with that excitement. I have heard, and have preserved with my pen, some few examples which have survived by mere accidents of memory in the repertoires of experienced and trained ballad-singers, and even as I set down these reminiscences my mind is invaded by certain remembered scraps of local song, such as

> The beans was in the oven
> She'd baked the night before,

a grim suggestion of the continuance of normal conditions in a household after its mistress has been struck down by the swift red hand of murder. When I encountered this ballad, years ago, I was still in that unregenerate state in which popular ballads are occasionally heard and applauded as excellent samples of unconscious humor, so that I can not with certainty pursue my quotation; but last summer I copied down from the singing of the Widow Palmer a Murder Ballad, or more properly a Manslaughter Ballad, which is so brief and in its concluding admonition so instructive withal that I can well afford to quote it in full. I have been unable to discover the event which lies back of it, and the Widow, exhibiting some petulance at my curiosity and inquiring with a touch of asperity what I saw about this particular song that was so very strange, could lend me no assistance. But it bears the marks of local origin, and as a local song I present it. The title is "McLellan's Son."

> It was on September the eighteenth day
>
> .   .   .   .   .
>
> A gun was heard, a mournful sound,
> Like thunder rolled and shook the ground.
>
> The people crowded to the spot
> From which there came that mournful shock.
> And there in death's cold fetters bound
> A victim bleeding on the ground.

It's there they saw a man and gun
Who had this dreadful murder done.
With rolling eyes cast on the ground
He told the truth to all around.

"It's I took up this cursed gun
To snap it off in careless fun,
When this poor boy with spirits large
Came up the hill and met the charge.

"I'll tell you what I'd have you do.
Take this same gun and shoot me too.
Where shall I hide my guilty head?
I wish to God I too was dead.

"It's take poor Daniel on a door
And lay him on the bar-room floor.
Send for a justice very soon,
And let the jury fill the room."

The parents of this murdered boy
Has given up all hopes of joy,
To think their son to man had grown
To die by folly not his own.

Take warning, all you careless youths.
Be always sure to speak the truth.
Take warning by McLellan's son.
Mind how you trifle with a gun.

But the home-made ballad of Nova Scotia was inspired
by the tragedies of the ocean more often than by those of
the land. Sometimes it is an unlucky or merely uncom-
fortable voyage, and sometimes it is the ultimate catastrophe of a total wreck. In a peninsula where a large pro-

portion even of the villages are sea-ports, where the native industry used to be ship-building, and where the vessels were always, in part at least, manned by native crews, the adventures of the ships that went down to the sea were of paramount interest. It was a not uncommon thing for a gifted sailor to compose a song for his fellows narrating the events of a perilous voyage, and often the crew combined to build up, stanza by stanza from individual contributions, a commemorative song for the maiden voyage of a new ship. All such ballads are, of course, local and ephemeral, and they rarely survive except in chance fragments. The following account of an unhappy voyage will give a fair taste of their quality. It was sung for me by a veteran who remembered that it had been composed by Cale White of Maitland, one of the hard-pressed crew.

> Saint Patrick's day in sixty-five
>   From New York we set sail.
> Kind Providence did favor us
>   With a sweet and pleasant gale.
>
> We bore away from America,
>   As you shall understand;
> With courage brave we rode the waves,
>   Bound down to Newfoundland.
>
> When two days out, to our distress,
>   Our captain he fell sick,
> And scarcely was enabled
>   To show himself on deck.
>
> The fever raged, which made us fear
>   That death was near at hand.
> For Halifax we bore away,
>   Bound down to Newfoundland.

The land we made, but knew it not,
  For strangers we were all,
Our captain not being able
  To come on deck at all.

So we were all obliged again
  To have her off from land.
With saddest hearts we put to sea,
  Bound down to Newfoundland.

All that night we ran our brig
  Till early the next day,
Our captain getting worse, we all
  With one accord did say:

"We'll square away for Cape Canso.
  My boys, now bear a hand."
In Arishat that afternoon we anchored safe
  Bound down to Newfoundland.

Unto the board of health we then
  For medical aid did go.
Our captain near the point of death
  That symptoms it did show.

The small-pox now was breaking out,
  For that it proved to be.
And eight days after we arrived,
  At God's just command,
He breathed his last in Arishat
  Bound down to Newfoundland.

Both day and night may we lament
  For our departed friend,
And pray to be protected
  From what has been his end.

Be with us and protect us, God,
  By thy almighty hand,
And guide us safe while on the seas
  Bound down to Newfoundland.

This is a sample of the sort of rough chronicle ballad that was not infrequently produced by a sailor or officer of poetic tendencies who had played his part in the events of an ill-fated voyage. It has the air of robust veracity and realism which one might expect from an active participant, and presents an interesting contrast to the more literary attempts of the landsman who celebrates in song the mere climax of a voyage which has ended in disaster. The ballad of the Cedar Grove, a steamer wrecked years ago off Cape Canso, has this effect of an embellished account from a person who has obtained his information through inquiry rather than through hard personal experience.

It's of a noble steamer,
  The Cedar Grove by name;
She crossed the briny ocean,
  From London city came.

She was strongly built on the banks of Clyde,
  Five hundred tons or more,
But her strength it proved of no avail
  On the rocks of Canso shore.

The night was dark and stormy,
  The lookout at his post;
The first he saw of danger
  Was breakers on the coast.

THE QUEST OF THE BALLAD

The signal it was given
    The engines to reverse,
"To starboard your helm!" the captain cries,
    "Our ship is off her course."

But still our noble steamer
    She nobly boomed along,
Till in one moment a dreadful crash
    Brought fear to every one.

Two engineers and firemen
    Were hard to work below,
And by their perseverance
    It's backward she did go.

Once more we gained the deep water,
    But yet our doom was sealed.
The briny waves rolled in her bows,
    And then to port she keeled.

With a heavy weight of water,
    From forward it did flow,
And into aft compartments,
    And down our ship did go.

The saddest of my story
    Which yet it doth remain,
We had one lady passenger,
    Miss Farrel was her name.

For to visit some relations
    In the city of St. John
She ventured on the briny deep,
    But now she's dead and gone.

A sailor said he saw her
  In the cabin door stand by,
Did grieve his heart with pity
  To hear her weep and cry.

He offered to console her,
  And said, "You'll not be lost,"
And a moment later that lady's form
  In the breaking waves was tossed.

Our steward held her bravely
  Out o'er the ship's dark rail,
And waiting for the boats
  To pull up against the gale,

A giant wave swept over
  Which did prevail his grip,
And then that lady's tender form
  Went floating from the ship.

The same wave took our captain,
  And he was seen no more.
Through heavy mist and darkness
  The boats still lingered near.

Two engineers were also lost
  Just as the ship went down.
Their bodies or the lady's
  Have never yet been found.

And now the ill-fated Cedar Grove
  On the bottom she doth lie.
To save the most of her cargo
  The divers hard did try.

A disfigured body
  Was carefully sent on,
Our agèd honored captain
  Who died while in command.

Our cargo was for Halifax,
  From the city of St. John,
And to the latter port
  Our steamer did belong.

She was strongly built on the banks of Clyde,
  Five hundred tons or more,
But her strength it proved of no avail
  On the rocks of Canso shore.

It is not impossible, of course, that the unknown author of "The Cedar Grove" may have been one of the participants in the tragic event, but in spite of a steady recurrence of the possessive "our" the ballad has the appearance of a landsman's composition. It has the merit of being a tolerably restrained narrative, with no very obvious attempts to destroy the hearer's peace of mind or even to lure the kindly moisture from his eye. But, somehow, the slightly overwrought incident of the "lady passenger" looms large before me. It is a sinister reminder of other ballads where the tale itself gasps and chokes and grows all but inarticulate in an atmosphere impregnated with sentimentality, and Nova Scotia has produced what may be accepted, in the absence of any rival hitherto discovered, as the roof and crown of the ballads of this type. About half a century ago a passenger ship named the Atlantic was split on a great rock off Prospect Point on the south shore of Nova Scotia, and the harrowing consequences, which by reason of later events we are enabled to realize very intimately, are detailed with unctuous fidelity by a local bard in a ballad of precisely fifty stanzas. The ballad was printed on broadside sheets and distributed far and wide throughout the province. Today there is not a single copy in existence, or if there is it has at least been successful in eluding my search. There are plenty of people in Nova Scotia who have dim recollections of the shipwreck, and there are some who can quote scraps of the ballad, but the only person I ever found who could sing it throughout was old Bob Langille, who by a prodigious feat of memory had mastered it so completely that he was able to sit down and, without any preliminary warning, sing the whole fifty stanzas to me without break or pause. I have shown that Bob was not one who carried his precious ballads on his sleeve for daws to peck at. For aught I know it may have been months or even years since he had sung it before, and if I quote a few preliminary stanzas the reader, who will be graciously pleased to bear in mind that the full tale is fifty, may have some conception of what it used to mean to be a ballad-singer.

> Dear friends, come listen to the tale,
>   The loss which we deplore
> Of the gallant ship Atlantic lost
>   On Nova Scotia's shore.
>
> The most terrific accident
>   Befell that fated ship
> As she approached those rocky shores
>   On her way across the deep.

THE QUEST OF THE BALLAD

The sun had set behind the hills,
    Night spread her wings around,
A night that will remembered be
    For many a year to come.

Alas, a ship, a noble ship,
    That had the ocean crossed,
And on the lonely Prospect shore
    That night was wrecked and lost.

With full a thousand souls on board
    Her captain had no fear,
And heeded not the rocky coast
    Which he was drawing near.

Till oh, alas, it was too late.
    The final shock was given.
That noble ship had struck the rock.
    Amidships she was riven.

The terror-stricken souls on board
    Oh, who could give them aid?
Unto each other looked for help,
    Each praying to be saved.

Numbers overboard were washed
    And perished in the deep.
While others, frozen with the cold,
    Died on the sinking ship.

Poor helpless women down below,
    Of whom not one was saved,
Dear little children too,
    All met a watery grave.

It was fortunate for Bob that no irascible host was present to stint him of his tale with the agonized cry, "No more of this, for goddes dignitee!" Chaucer should have ended his tale of Sir Thopas in peace if I had been his audience, for I sat without sound or moan while Bob proceeded through one decade after another of this vague and lugubrious narrative. The nameless bard of "The Wreck of the Atlantic" had one fierce and relentless purpose while he composed, to rend his hearers with an uncontrollable anguish of sobbing, and he varied his mode of attack with a cunning equal to his ferocity. Here is one of his episodes:

> Amongst the women there were two
>   Who down the waves that night
> Had each of them a little babe
>   That scarce had seen the light.
>
> A lady with her babe in arms
>   Had reached the deck, we're told,
> With nothing but her night-clothes on
>   To shield her from the cold.
>
> To save her life her slender form
>   Was fastened to a mast,
> Where ten long hours she there remained
>   Before she breathed her last.
>
> And ere she died her little babe
>   Was swept into the sea.
> What misery did that mother bear
>   In her hours of agony!

The reader will note that he is craftily invited, in this last stanza, to permit his imagination to dwell upon those

aspects of the situation which have not been clearly outlined by the poet himself. A little later the poet suddenly
realizes, with a white and consuming rage, that this invitation may have been declined or ignored, and with that
thought he abandons the pitfall and the mine and charges
upon us with open and declared frightfulness.

> One Mr. Street, a gentleman,
>   Quite frantic with despair,
> From cabin came, and in his arms
>   His little daughter bare.
>
> And to one Ellery he said,
>   "Pray Charlie, take my child
> That I may go my wife to seek,
>   The billows raging wild."
>
> And as the steward gazed on the child
>   And saw her face so fair,
> His thoughts went quickly to his home.
>   He had one like her there.
>
> The father did the mother seek,
>   But neither one came back.
> The angry waves soon swept them off
>   From off the sinking wreck.
>
> Poor suffering little innocent,
>   It cried, "Papa, come!"
> Its clothes were then just taken from
>   Its little bed so warm.
>
> It cried "Papa!" a short time,
>   But Papa never came,
> Expiring in the stewards arms
>   In agony and pain.

Its little soul to heaven flew
  To call its papa there.
I hope they hand in hand will walk
  Through heavenly mansions fair.

After this we have left only one defense, and the chances
are that in our despair we shall take to it with craven
alacrity. At least, we frantically assure ourselves, we
were not in this frightful wreck; we are even now sitting
comfortably about on our chairs listening to a mere tale of
old unhappy far-off things. But the cunning bard has
foreseen this cowardly subterfuge long before it has entered into our slow and now half-benumbed consciousness.
Sallying from an ambush which he has carefully prepared
he executes a swift and dexterous flank movement which
hurries us all to one fearful and irrevocable doom.

With all our friends around us
  We close our eyes in sleep.
Our thoughts will often wander
  Across the dreary deep,

In grief for those who closed their eyes.
  No thoughts of death were near.
But to wake a sinking in the deep,
  Shrieks sounding in their ears.

So it is with us, my loving friends,
  There's breakers all around.
And in an unexpected hour
  The last great trump will sound.

The shrieks and groans and cries of those
  Who fear the chastening rod
All unprepared must then come forth
  To meet Almighty God.

Let me hasten to the rescue of the gentle and stricken reader. He has never, at least, been a dastardly mutineer. He has never conspired with his base comrades to murder an unsuspecting captain and mate and throw them over-board, nor has he—and now allow me to offer my con-gratulations to a smiling and complacent reader—been captured and tried for his crime and hanged upon the gal-lows tree in full view of a righteously appeased populace. Furthermore, he can feel quite sure that never will he be hanged for that particular offence. And now, if the reader has not grown too self-important to take an interest in my homely activities I shall proceed, under his regal scrutiny, to tack my clumsy bark through the laboring seas of my proposed tale.

When I was a small boy in the happy purlieus of my father's house one of my daily associates was the gardener John Jollimore. Some day I hope I shall rise to the great task of depicting John as he truly was, but it is neither within my power nor within the scope of my narrative that I should do so now. For the present I am permitted only to mention him as the person who introduced my quivering youthful mind to the terrific tale of the mutiny and whole-sale murder on the good ship Saladin.

John was a man of superb and preternatural solemnity, which is not to say that he was no humorist. He had, in his own queer original way, a very pretty wit and a well conceived manner of humorous speech. But neither his own wit nor that of his neighbor, not even a practical joke itself, could break that musing saturnine face into smiles. On three occasions only have I beheld him writhing in the clutch of laughter. On each of these occasions my boyish mind was harrowed with amazement, and even now my mature wisdom can only vaguely link these effects to their unnatural causes. The first was when, leaning upon his garden rake and gazing down upon my small recumbent form in the grass, he told the circumstantial narrative of a gross insult to his wife. The second was when he described with equal faithfulness the tragic death of his beloved dog Briskinardo (so named, I need hardly explain, by John himself) through the awkwardness of his myopic friend Jacob Joudry, who was helping him to fell a tree. And the third was when he told me the story of the mutiny on the Saladin.

It was on a dark winter evening when my cousin and I had met to work out together our lesson in the Latin accidence for the next day's recitation, and had in pursuance of that scholarly design repaired secretly to John's cottage, that I first heard the story of the mutiny. John's imagination always burned most hotly after the set of the sun. Sometimes, in those fervid periods, he would be wholly given over to an exposition of demonology and witchcraft, supporting his beliefs with ample illustration out of his personal knowledge; sometimes he yielded himself to the fascination of murder and of mysterious nocturnal death; and sometimes he roused himself to a consideration of stupendous mechanical devices for accruing fabulous wealth, such as an improvised cannon that would bring down a whole flock of wild geese at one shot or an arrangement of nets that would infallibly catch every fish in the river in one night. On the evening in question he was pondering darkly in the chimney-corner when we arrived, and the subject of his thoughts, as presently appeared, was the old Saladin story.

The tale as I am to tell it presently is gathered from

more authentic sources than this, but in my own mind it will always take its peculiar color from its first appearance in my consciousness. The Saladin songs, also, I gathered years afterward in fairly complete versions, while John's recital was a mere piecing up of broken verses; but it will be long till I forget his rendition of two stanzas, incoherently brought together, as I have since ascertained, from two of the songs, but coherent enough in their suggestion of the bloody event.

> We shed the blood of innocence,
>   The same I don't deny.
> We washed our hands in human blood,
>   For which we now must die.
>
> O first we killed our captain,
>   And then we killed our mate,
> Then overboard the bos'n threw
>   Together in the deep.

This was harrowing enough to the imaginations of two dishonest schoolboys who were presently to make their stealthy way home through the blackness of a dreary winter night, but John, securely housed in his own cottage till daylight should come, did not fear to give rein to his fantasy. "My God, boys," he entreated us, "jist think o' that deck with the dead bodies strewed onto it an' all red an' slippery with blood!" Then, for some reason which it would be idle to try to explain, he burst into an astounding fit of monstrous laughter.

Since I am now to proceed to the Saladin tale itself I shall have to dismiss John from my active consciousness, for his account of the great crime is only one of many distorted and incomplete versions which I have heard at various times. I shall henceforth be chiefly guided by the ballads, which were composed while the event was still fresh gossip in Nova Scotia, and by the evidence of the condemned mutineers at their trial in Halifax.

On the 28th day of April, in the year 1844, a barque with sails set and royals flying, stranded herself on a ledge of rock off Country Harbour on the south coast of Nova Scotia. The fishermen of the region pushed out in great excitement and found the vessel securely hung up on the reef. The legend on her stern proclaimed that she was the Saladin, hailing from Newcastle, England, and at her prow was a handsome figure-head representing the Sultan for whom she was named. Proceeding on board they discovered a state of affairs which partly accounted for the insane and blindfold haste which had driven the barque at a reef on a fair day and under full sail. The Saladin was manned by six sailors only, and one of them had a wooden leg and was therefore of no use except for odd jobs about the deck. There was not an officer on board, and the explanations offered by the seamen for this and other sinister circumstances were so incoherent that the visitors decided to take the scanty crew into custody and send word to Halifax. Affairs moved slowly in those days, but before long a guard arrived and the arrested seamen were taken to Halifax and placed on trial. In the course of the proceedings that followed it transpired that four of the men had been guilty of concerted mutiny and of a series of murders in which the other two had been made unwilling partners. The whole affair aroused the most excited interest throughout Nova Scotia. A series of ballads, purporting to tell the tale from the various angles of the respective criminals, grew up as the trial proceeded. So long as ballad-singing maintained its position among the popular entertainments these were sung at the homely firesides through the length and breadth of the province, and to this day one may occasionally hear some village council disputing the gruesome details around a blacksmith's forge and summoning reluctant stanzas and lines from the vanishing ballads to serve as evidence. I shall now go back to the beginning of the tale as it shows through the criminal records, and when the plot thickens I shall permit the ballads to play their part in the sombre recital.

Near the end of the year 1843 the ill-starred barque sailed from Newcastle on her last outward trip. She was bound for Valparaiso, and was commanded by Alexander Mackenzie, reputed even in those days of absolute shipmasters to be a cruel and tyrannous captain. During the long voyage out the crew received ample and continued evidence of the truth of these rumors, and on their arrival at Valparaiso some of them deserted.

For the homeward voyage the barque was loaded with several hundred tons of guano, seventy tons of copper, and about a ton of silver in bars of a hundred and fifty pounds. In addition to the cargo the captain received for transportation about nine thousand dollars in specie and some packets of letters and papers for the Admiralty in London. Finally, the depleted ranks of the crew were filled in with sailors "sharked up" in the usual way at Valparaiso. When she left port the Saladin was manned by the following crew: James Allen, Samuel Collins, Thomas Moffat, William Travascus (alias Johnston), John Hazleton, and Charles Andersen. These were the men who sailed before the mast. The first three, whose names will not appear again, and who themselves were destined to a present and melancholy disappearance, served on the captain's watch. The other three, whom we shall have ample cause to mention again, were on the mate's watch, and in their company we shall find George Jones, a disabled seaman with a wooden leg, who was working his way home as a sail-maker. The cook and steward were, respectively, William Carr and John Galloway. The first mate was Thomas Byerley. The second mate, who was also ship's carpenter, is mentioned only as one of the first to be murdered and thrown overboard.

So much for the constitution of the officers and crew, but the central figure in the crime has yet to be introduced. When the ship was loading in Valparaiso Captain Mackenzie contracted a friendship with a man who is described as "a fiend in human shape." This was Captain Fielding, ex-smuggler, ex-pirate, and perpetual villain. His vessel, the Victory, had been seized at some port on the Pacific coast for smuggling and other illicit traffic, and he was now in Valparaiso with his son waiting for something to turn up. He learned of the rich cargo that was being shipped on board the Saladin, and with that in view presented himself to Mackenzie as a destitute brother-captain desirous of returning to England. Mackenzie, who with all his hotness and irascibility seems to have been a generous and singularly unsuspicious person, at once granted the pair a free passage home. The ballad of Charles Gustav (or Augustus) Andersen introduces this arch-plotter in a burst of remorseful recollection.

> They shipped me on board the Saladin,
>   As you shall understand.
> She was bound for Valparaiso.
>   Mackenzie had command.

We arrived there in safety
    Without the least delay,
Till Fielding came on board of her.
    Curse on that fatal day!

'Twas Fielding who induced us
    To do that horrid crime.
We might have prevented it
    If we had thought in time.

We shed the blood of innocence,
    The same I don't deny.
We washed our hands in human blood,
    For which we have to die.

Fielding's plan was to get control of the ship and her cargo, and to this end he worked steadily and patiently from the day they put to sea. His chief ally in this enterprise was the unsuspecting captain himself, who lost no opportunity to make himself hated and feared by his crew. Jones, the crippled sail-maker, was the first to come under Fielding's influence, and at his trial he testified that he had repelled Fielding's first advances and had tried to warn the captain, who had refused to listen and had blasphemously ordered him to get back to his work. The next to be won over was Hazleton. Travascus soon followed, and now the only man strictly necessary to complete the group was the young Swede Andersen, the remaining member of the mate's watch. Andersen seems to have been an honest youth with little taste for treasons and stratagems, and it was quite possible that he might have been the effective barrier in the way of the conspirators; but at the opportune time the cynical gods inspired Captain Mackenzie to leap upon him while he was doing duty at the helm and beat him severely for no apparent good reason. The conspirators offered him his revenge, and he accepted the offer.

The Saladin had sailed from Valparaiso on the 8th day of February. Two months had passed while Fielding was slowly and cautiously mustering his forces for the mutiny, and the barque was now heading up along the east coast of South America about two degrees north of the equator. The conspirators arranged to strike their blow on the night of the 13th of April during the mate's watch—that is, when they would normally be serving their turn on deck and when the other seamen would be in their bunks. Jones, the crippled sail-maker, was of course on neither watch, and it was arranged that the signal for starting the activity should be his appearance on deck. Then under the leadership of Fielding they were to proceed to murder the officers and the sailors of the captain's watch. For some reason, however, Jones failed to appear that night, and nothing was done. Next day Fielding managed to get a secret interview with Jones, who had apparently been overcome by fear, and rated him so bitterly for his cowardice that when the following night came around he took the easier way and gave the appointed signal. Then the four mutineers, led by Fielding, and armed with knives, proceeded aft to the cabin to begin the night's work.

> On the fourteenth night of April,
>   I am sorry to relate,
> We began the desperate enterprise
>   By killing first the mate.

> And then we killed the carpenter,
>   And overboard them threw;
> The captain next we put to death,
>   And three more of the crew.

The watch were in their hammocks
  When the work of death begun.
They were all killed as they came up.
  We killed them one by one.

These poor unhappy victims
  Lay in their beds asleep,
We called them up and murdered them
  And threw them in the deep.

As the ballad indicates, the mutineers, after murdering
the officers (the carpenter, it will be remembered, was also
the second mate) proceeded forward and called out the
sleeping sailors one by one, striking them down as they
emerged on deck. Carr and Galloway, the cook and steward, were still below, but becoming alarmed at the noise
of scuffling, they now barricaded themselves and refused
to come out, and the mutineers finally agreed to spare
them on condition that they should take an oath of secrecy.
Then, their labors crowned with success, the whole party
retired to the cabin, where Fielding made each man swear
on the Bible that he would maintain inviolate secrecy and
fidelity to the cause; after which, as a practical demonstration of good faith, he collected the axes, revolvers, and
knives, and ostentatiously threw them overboard.

Fielding's plan for utilizing the treasure on board had
been carefully thought out, and he now revealed it to his
followers. He himself was a skilful and experienced
navigator, and it so happened that he was thoroughly familiar with the eastern coast and waters of Canada. He
proposed, therefore, to strike north to a lonely part of the
west coast of Newfoundland, conceal the treasure there,
scuttle the ship in deep water, take to the long-boat and

sail up the river St. Lawrence to a place of safety, and there abide quietly until people should cease to speculate on the mysterious disappearance of the Saladin. Then they would secure a small coasting vessel and return to Newfoundland for the treasure.

> It was on a Sunday morning,
>   The work of death was done,
> When Fielding took the Bible
>   And swore us every one.
>
> The tempting prize before his eyes
>   He kept it still in view,
> And like a band of brothers
>   We were sworn to be true.
>
> "Our firearms and weapons
>   We'll all throw in the deep,
> And then we'll steer for Newfoundland
>   If prevailing winds will keep.
>
> "And secrete all our treasures there
>   In some secluded place."
> Had it not been for his treachery
>   That might have been the case.

The last two lines of my quotation carry the hint of a new and sinister complication. This "treachery" for which the doomed sailors thus bitterly reproach Fielding in retrospect seems to have been with him an instinct so persistent and compelling that, "like the villain in the old play," he was bound sooner or later to lose himself in the mazes of his own tortuous schemes. A day or two after the new régime had been established he gave orders that Carr and

Galloway, the cook and steward, should sleep in the forecastle, and suggested to his fellow-murderers that these two men could now be disposed of in the familiar way. But his men balked at this proposal. They had supped full with horrors, and had no appetite for more. It may well have struck them that this cold-blooded leader must have been planning no less complete a program than the gradual elimination of all his associates and the full possession of the treasure. Whether it was this, or whether there was something vaguely menacing in Fielding's attitude towards them, at any rate they began vehemently to suspect him, and Travascus was secretly deputed to find an opportunity to search the cabin. The search revealed a brace of pistols and a knife carefully concealed among Fielding's belongings. There could now be no doubt as to their leader's ultimate intent, and after a hurried consultation the men rushed upon Fielding and his son and fettered them securely with ropes. Carr and Galloway were accomplices in this new mutiny, and as they were the only ones who had not yet "washed their hands in human blood" they were elected to throw the two victims overboard.

> We found with Captain Fielding,
>   For which he lost his life,
> A brace of loaded pistols,
>   Likewise a carving knife.
>
> We suspected him of treachery,
>   Which did enrage the crew.
> He was seized by Carr and Galloway,
>   And overboard was threw.

His son cried out for mercy,
He being left alone.
But his entreaty was cut off.
There was no mercy shown.

We served him like his father
Who found a watery grave,
For we buried son and father
Beneath the briny wave.

The immediate peril was now disposed of; but it is the way of plots to thicken as they proceed, and even now "this even-handed justice" was extending to the wretched mutineers their own poisoned chalice to drain to its last dregs. Fielding had been at least an intelligent and inventive leader and a skilful navigator, and now there was no man left in the company who had more than an elementary knowledge of navigation. Galloway the steward knew a little more than the others, and he was, in default of a better, elected to Fielding's place. They knew of no likelier scheme than the one which their dead leader had outlined, and though not one of them had the slightest knowledge of the northern coast they kept on their supposed course for Newfoundland. Their one desperate need now was to get the whole business over quickly, and they crowded upon the staggering barque every inch of canvas that she would carry. The first murders, it will be remembered, had taken place on the night of the 14th of April, and about two degrees north of the equator. On the 28th day of the same month the Saladin, after a remarkably swift passage, came within sight of her ultimate sea-mark on the south shore of Nova Scotia. The sailors supposed that they were nearing their appointed goal on the coast of Newfoundland, and in their haste to find anchoring ground well inshore they drove their hard-pressed barque full tilt upon the reef.

> We sailed the ship before the wind,
>   As we could do no more,
> And on the twenty-eighth of April
>   Were shipwrecked on the shore.
>
> We were all apprehended
>   And into prison cast,
> Tried and were found guilty,
>   And sentence on us passed.
>
> Four of us are now condemned
>   And ready for to die,
> And the day of execution
>   Is the thirtieth of July.

At the trial in Halifax both Carr and Galloway turned Queen's evidence. They had not been in the original conspiracy, the part that they had played in the second killing had been thrust upon them by their comrades, and it could hardly be accounted to them for unrighteousness that they had been the slayers of Fielding. At any rate they were acquitted. Andersen, Jones, Travascus, and Hazelton were hanged on the 30th of July, 1844, upon a gallows erected on the South Common in Halifax, and in the last scene of this humble tragedy Jones the sail-maker stumped out upon his wooden leg to the front of the scaffold and addressed the throng of spectators, avowing his guilt and solemnly adjuring the young men to take warning from the bitter example which was now to be consummated before their eyes.

If I have dwelt at exceeding length upon the melancholy details which form the background of the Saladin songs I have done so because I have found in this episode a rare opportunity to demonstrate the relationship which pretty constantly exists between the popular ballad and the actual incident from which it springs. It is not always, of course, that the ballad grows so directly and contemporaneously out of the fact as it does in this case. Frequently it displays beside the fact certain of those supernatural and legendary accretions which so quickly attach themselves to a tale on its oral round, but its avowed aim is to present a true story of an important incident seen from a point of view as near as may be to that incident. In the composition of the simple and dignified ballads of an older period this anxiety, as we all know, precluded the introduction of any specious kind of ornamentation. The bare story was allowed to rest on its own merits, and the reader need only turn back to the versions which I have quoted of "Little Musgrave" and of "Lord Thomas and Fair Ellinor" to realize afresh how great those merits were. But, unhappily, the literary movement which in the eighteenth century introduced sentimentalism as the approved atmosphere in which to view unhappy and tragic occurrences ultimately worked down to the humblest order of poets, and in the nineteenth century few tragic ballads were composed which did not clothe the event in a flaunting suit of gratuitous mourning. Of the Saladin songs the worst in this respect is the one narrating the episode from the point of view of Charles Augustus (or Gustav) Andersen. The Jones ballad, from which I have freely quoted in my narrative of the mutiny, is a comparatively severe account of the event, but in the lachrymose confes-

,sion of Charles Augustus one catches only rare glimpses of narration floating like drift-wood upon the surface of a turbid sea of sensibility; and the humble bosom has in a degenerate age become so attuned to the tearful appeal that this is the particular Saladin ballad that has been singled out for widest popularity. It may be instructive to place it now against the somber background of the unadorned tale as I have related it:

Come all ye human countrymen, with pity lend an ear
And hear my feeling story. You can't but shed a tear.
I'm here in close confinement, bound down in irons strong,
Surrounded by strong granite walls and sentenced to be
     hung.

Charles Augustus Andersen is my right and proper name.
Since I came to custody I ne'er denied the same.
I came of decent parents although I die in scorn.
Believe me now I much lament that ever I was born.

My father was a shipwright. I might have been the same.
He taught me good examples. To him I leave no blame.
Likewise my tender mother for me did suffer sore.
When she hears the sad announcement I'm sure she'll
     suffer more.

O dear and loving mother, if I could see your face
I'd kiss your lips with tenderness and take your last em-
     brace.
I'd bathe you in my tears of grief before my final hour.
I'd then submit myself to God, his holy will and power.

Farewell, sisters and brothers that's dear unto me,
So far beyond the ocean whose face I ne'er can see.
Those happy days I spent with you upon my native shore!
Farewell, sweet Uddivalla, I ne'er shall see you more.

If I could recall those days again how happy I should be
To live at home among my friends in love and unity.
When I think of former innocence and those I left behind
'Tis God and him alone that knows the horrors of my mind.

No books of consolation are here that I can read,
I profess the Church of England. By nation I'm a Swede.
Those words that are addressed to me I can't well under-
stand,
So I must die like a heathen all in a foreign land.

'Twas in the town of Gothenburg where I was bred and
born.
Here in the city of Halifax I end my days in scorn.
O pity my misfortunes and warning take by me
To shun all bad company and beware of mutiny.

Since I left my tender parents 'tis but four years ago,
This awful fate awaited me, but little did I know.
I got into bad company, which has inducèd me
To become a murderer and a pirate on the sea.

They shipped me on board the Saladin, as you will under-
stand.
She was bound for Valparaiso. Mackenzie had command.
We arrived there in safety without the least delay,
Till Fielding came on board of her. Curse on that fatal
day!

'Twas Fielding who induced us to do that horrid crime.
We might have prevented it if we had thought in time.
We shed the blood of innocence, the same I don't deny,
We stained our hands in human blood for which we have
to die.

225

O Lord, I fear your vengeance. Your judgment much
    I dread,
To appear before your judgment seat with hands imbrued
    in blood.
I fear your indignation. Your pardon still I crave.
Dear Lord, have mercy on my soul beyond the gloomy
    grave.

The sheriff and his officers all came to him in jail.
He knew the fate awaited him, but never seemed to fail.
They placed the final halter on to end all shame and strife.
With his own hand he greased the cord that cut the thread
    of life.

They led him to a lonely spot and to that awful stand.
He viewed the briny ocean and then the pleasant land.
The rope of justice slipped the ring, which quickly stopped
    his breath.
Thus ended his career in the violent pains of death.

The Saladin songs, by reason of their rich background
of attested fact, mark the high-water limit of interest in
Nova Scotian production, and I shall not precipitate an
anti-climax by returning to examples of such unattached
song as I considered earlier in the chapter. It seems quite
possible, even to me, that I have found in this combination of song, tale, and legal record more interest than it
intrinsically possesses, but the conviction of such bias I
should receive without shame. Very early in life I came
under the spell of singers and narrators who wove the story
into my personal experience as effectively as if I myself
had been a cabin-boy on the ill-starred barque, and in recent years I have speculated many a time on the dark
events which must lie behind those century-old ballads of
the folk just as the true tales of Jones, Hazleton, Travascus, and Andersen lie behind the Saladin songs.

CHAPTER TEN

THE DECLINE OF BALLAD-SINGING

The mournful truth that most constantly obtrudes itself upon the collector is that the oral propagation of ballads has in our day and generation almost ceased. And I, for my part, have taken a rather special interest in attempting to discover the causes that have conspired to bring about this condition in my chosen field. My chief source of information has been the scattered band of hoary-haired singers who still remember the days when ballad-singing was a dignified means for entertaining a respectable company, and not, as it now is, the chance possession of a few queer old people who continue to dishonor their gray locks by chanting songs that up-to-date people have no time or inclination to listen to. From these witnesses I have gathered evidence, in scattered bits, which has all pointed to the conclusion that those processes which in the old country have taken centuries in the working out have in Nova Scotia proceeded from the beginning to the end in the course of three or four generations. A brief consideration of the downfall of ballad-singing in Nova Scotia will therefore present, in miniature, a very suggestive picture of the larger movement of folk-lore towards its decline and fall.

The first witness that I shall select is old James Isaac Macdonald, a Scotch Nova Scotian whom I discovered some five years ago while wandering up and down upon the earth in pursuit of ballad-lore. When I made the acquaintance of James Isaac he was living in Tatamagouche, a sea-port town on the north shore of Nova Scotia; but he had been born, and had spent the first forty years—that is, the first half—of his life at the West River, an inland district peopled by Scotch settlers. During his early days at the West River ballad-singing had been in full swing, and he himself, as he proudly averred, had been one of the most gifted of the singers. From this high estate he had long since fallen, but there still remained, in the unused corners of his mind, some recollections that will serve to illuminate the tragical history of the popular ballad.

The West River district was settled, during the latter half of the eighteenth century, by Scotch people, some from the Highlands and some from the Lowlands. Through the first half of the nineteenth century new settlers kept arriving, and thus the people of the district were kept in pretty close touch with the parent country. James Isaac's parents came out about 1820, and according to his account they sang innumerable songs of old Scotland, some of them recorded on broadside sheets which were carefully treasured in the family. Also, as far back as he could remember, his parents "kept the Post-Office" at the West River,—which means simply that the mails were brought to their house for distribution—and he had a clear recollection of the occasional arrival of newly-printed broadsides from the old country, for his own family and for other people in the community.

It meant something to have a store of ballads at one's command in those days. The old man grew large and bland with complacency as he recounted to me an occasion when he had squarely established his supremacy in a big ballad-contest, which came about in the following way.

One winter, when he was a young man, he rode down to Pictou to take the boat for Charlottetown, which is situated on the opposite side of the Northumberland Strait. A storm came up, the boat could not leave at the appointed time, and James Isaac was compelled to take refuge at an inn along with a group of travellers whose journey had also been interrupted. After supper it was proposed that the tedium of the evening should be relieved by a "singing-match," to last until one of the company should stand out as undisputed champion. So the contest began, one singer matching another until long after midnight, when everybody was "sung out" except James Isaac and a resourceful stranger from the south shore. The latter held out for some time longer, but finally was driven to admit that he had reached his last song. Then did James Isaac proceed to bear his unblushing honors thick upon him. "What, man!" he cried to his fallen adversary, in a craftily-assumed tone of surprise, "Don't say ye're through already! Why, God bless me, I hae fifty more on the tip o' me tongue!"

This was a tale of doughty deeds performed in the far distant past. When I encountered old James Isaac Macdonald he had no fifty ballads on the tip of his tongue, and the story of his downfall is this. When about forty years old he had moved to Tatamagouche, a sea-port town peopled by descendants of English, Scotch, and French settlers; and as he had a fair education for his day, and a strong ambition to entertain in any way that might be acceptable to his neighbors, he soon became reasonably prominent in the social life of the community. Ballad-singing was now becoming an antiquated and scarcely respectable performance, especially in such a community as

229

Tatamagouche, where, as I shall explain later, social influences were operating that were inimical to the life and growth of folk-lore. James Isaac, though he never thought of despising the ballads he had once held so dear, naturally enough permitted himself to forget all about them, and turned his attention to the sort of music in vogue among the people whom he wished to entertain. I procured only three or four ballads from him, all of them in more or less battered condition. The one that he remembered best was "The Blaeberry Courtship," a tale of the prosperous suitor who disguises himself as a humble peasant in order to win the hand of his chosen lass through his own unaided attractions. The ballad was long and involved, but James Isaac had retained his grip on it through the years of neglect because one of his friends at the West River had been very fond of it and had always asked him to sing it for her on his visits to his former home. This friend was an old Scotchwoman who had left the Highlands in her girlhood; and if I present the ballad which so vividly recalled for her the blaeberries and the heather of her native mountains the reader will easily understand her eagerness to nourish it during the long years of her sojourn in a foreign land.

THE BLAEBERRY COURTSHIP

"Will ye gang to the Highlands, my jewel, wi' me?
Will ye gang to the Highlands my flock for to see?
It is health to my jewel to breathe the fresh air
And to pu' the blaeberries in the forest sae fair."

"In the Highlands, my jewel, I'll no gang wi' thee,
For the road it is lang and hills they are hie,
For I love these low valleys and the sweet corn-fields
Before all the blaeberries your wild mountains yields."

THE DECLINE OF BALLAD-SINGING

"O the hills are bonny where the heather's in bloom;
'Twould cheer a fine fancy in the month o' June
To pu' the blaeberries and carry them home
And set them on your table when December comes on."

Then up spake the faither, that saucy old man,
"Ye might a chosen a mistress amang ye're ain clan.
It's but poor entertainment for our lowland dames
For to promise them berries when the wild heather blooms.

"Take up ye're green plaidie, walk over yon hill,
For the sight o' your Highland face does me much ill.
I'll wed my own daughter and spend pennies too,
To whom my heart pleases, and what's that to you?"

He called on his daughter, he gave her an advice,
Saying, "If ye'll gang wi' him I'm sure ye're not wise.
He's a poor Hielan' fellow, he's as poor as a crow,
Of the clan o' the Caterans for aught we may know.

"But if ye gang wi' him I'm sure ye'll gang bare.
Ye'll get naething that faither or mither can spare.
Of all ye possess I'll deprive ye for aye
If o'er the hills, lassie, ye gang away."

"Keep back ye're hand, faither, ye're no willin' to give,
But I'll fain go wi' him as sure as I live.
What signifies gold or treasure to me
When the Highland hills is 'tween my love and me?"

Now she's awa' wi' him in spite o' them a',
Awa' to a place which her eyes never saw.
He had no a steed for to carry her on,
But aye he said, "Lassie, think na the road long."

In a short time thereafter they cam to a glen.
The lass being weary, she sat hersen doon.
"Rise up, my brave lassie, and let us gang on.
For the sun will be gone doon before we get hame."

"My shoes are all torn and my feet are all rent,
I'm weary wi' travellin' and like to faint.
Were it not for the sake o' ye're kind companie
I wad lie in this desert until I wad dee."

In a short time thereafter they cam to a grove
Where the flocks they were feeding in numberless droves.
While Alan stood musing, his flocks for to see,
"Step on," said the lassie, "That's na pleasure to me."

Twa bonnie laddies wi' green tartan trews
And twa bonnie lassies were butting the yoes.
"Ye're welcome, honored master, ye're welcome again.
This while we've been lookin' for ye comin' hame."

"Put in your yoes, lassies, and gang awa hame.
I hae brought a swan frae the north to tame.
Her feathers are fallen, and where can she fly?
The best bed in all the house, there shall she lie."

The laddies did whistle and the laddies did sing,
And they made to the lassie a broad bed of down.
The lassie's heart was doon and couldna' well raise
Till mony a lad and lass came in wi' mony a phrase.

Early next morning he led her to the high,
And bad her look round her as far as she could spy.
"These lands and possessions—I have no debt to pay.
Ye scarce can walk round them in a long summer's day."

"O Alan, O Alan, I'm indebted to thee.
A debt, dear Alan, I never can pay.
O Alan, O Alan, how cam ye to me,
Sure I'm not worthy your bride for to be."

"Why call ye me Alan when Sandy's my name?
Why call ye me Alan? Ye're surely to blame.
For don't ye remember, when at school wi' me,
I was hated by all the rest, lovèd by thee?

"How aft have I fed on your bread and your cheese
When I had naething else but a handful o' peas.
Your hard-hearted faither did hunt me wi' dogs.
They rave all my bare heels and tore all my rags."

"Is this my dear Sandy whom I loved so dear?
I have not heard of you for mony a year.
When all the rest went to bed sleep was frae me
For thinkin' whatever had become o' thee."

"In love we began and in love we will end,
And in joy and mirth we will our days spend.
And a trip once more to your faither we'll go
To relieve the old farmer of his toil and woe."

Wi' men and maidservants to wait them upon,
Awa' in a chaise to her faither they've gone.
The laddie went foremost, that brave highland loon,
Till they cam to the gate that leads to the toon.

When they cam to the gate he gave a loud roar,
"Come doon, gentle farmer, Katherine's at your door!"
He looked out at the window and saw his daughter's face.
Wi' his hat in his hand he made a great phrase.

"Haud on your hat, faither, and don't let it fa'.
It's not for the peacock to bow to the craw."
"O haud your tongue, Sandy, and don't ye taunt me.
My daughter's nae worthy your bride for to be."

Then he's held the bridle reins until he cam doon,
And then he conveyed him into a fine room.
Wi' the best o' Scotch whiskey they drank o' a toast.
And the son and the faither drank baith in one glass.

In addition to the complete song thus fortuitously preserved in James Isaac's memory, there were snatches and
fragments of many sorts, dry bones which the old man
had neither interest nor inspiration to reanimate. As a
last resort I enquired about the ballad sheets which had
been held in such high esteem by his family, but he could
not account for one of them, nor did he seem in the least
disturbed by his failure to do so. Broadside sheets were
very useful in their day, but when ballad-singing went out
of fashion they were tossed aside like a yesterday's newspaper, and they disappeared just as surely and just as
quietly as the yesterday's newspapers do. It is very easy
to blame the careless possessors for their failure to become
imbued with an antiquarian zeal in exchange for the active
and contemporary interest which was ceasing to be a part
of their attitude toward the ballad, but to do so is entirely
unjust. When the change came they treated their ballads,
including broadside sheets when they happened to possess
them, as we treat our worn-out hats and coats and the
popular novels that we read with enthusiasm a year ago.

Thus we have as one reason for the decline of ballad-
singing in this representative district the influx of more
modern music and methods of entertainment, added to the

increasing suspicion that ballads were becoming old-fashioned and out-of-date. A second reason may receive preliminary illustration in one of the experiences of old Bob Langille. Bob, whose capacious memory was charged with ballads received through the regular channels of oral transmission, had had one tragic experience with a broadside sheet, a piece of paper containing the sentimental ballad of "The Wreck of the Atlantic," which I have discussed in an earlier chapter. He had, fortunately, procured the services of some "scholar" to read it for him while he committed it to memory, but the paper itself had been lost in a most irritating manner, and Bob went into a paroxysm of grief and rage as he told me about it. "When I think," said he, with a vain attempt to be calm, "of how I lost that ballat, I can't keep the tears out o' me eyes. John Forbes up the River was crazy to larn it, an' he got me to lend it to him fer jist two days. Then I didn't see him fer three weeks, when he comes ridin' along on his horse, an' thinkin' to git by the house without me seein' him. But I goes out on the road an' says, 'John Forbes,' says I, 'where's my ballat?' 'Bob,' says he, 'yer ballat's lost, but I'm willin' to pay ye fer it.' 'Ye damn' old scoundrel,' says I, 'If ye wasn't an old man I'd haul ye down off yer horse an' kick ye.'—"But," concluded Bob in a heart-broken tone, "I never seen me ballat* from that day to this."

The person who displayed this lively and extraordinary interest in the literature of an elder day was, as we have seen in an earlier chapter, an octogenarian who lived just

* It will be noticed that Bob consistently referred to the broadside sheet as a "ballat." This illustrates the terminology of all the people of his class. A ballad printed on a sheet is a "ballad" or "ballat," and a ballad known only through oral tradition is "an old song." Needless to say, one practically never encounters the former term. Printed ballads were circulated only in the rarest cases.

outside the village of Tatamagouche with two sisters only a trifle less ancient than himself. To him the ballads of centuries ago were as replete with interest as they had been to the simple folk of the community in the days before railroads and newspapers, and he had at all times an appreciative and harmonious audience in his two old sisters, who were also pleased to consider that the world had not yet advanced beyond the second quarter of the nineteenth century.

Bob's humble cottage was situated about a mile from the residence of that slave of fashion, James Isaac Macdonald. The two old men were about the same age, they were in a general way members of the same community, and in their younger days they had both been earnest and enthusiastic singers of popular ballads. Now, in their old age, I found one of them with his enthusiasm unabated, while the other had to ransack the dusty shelves of his memory to find even the names of a few of the ballads that he had sung many years ago.

I have already said that James Isaac was not one of those superior persons who consider the popular ballads quaint, old-fashioned, and absurdly naïve. He thought of them, on the contrary, as very good songs for the day in which they had flourished, and believed, not unnaturally, that they had disappeared before the advance of newer songs of a higher order of culture. His tone, when he referred to them, was neither enthusiastic nor supercilious, and he repeated or described them in so far as his memory would serve him, with the usual remark that they were "very good old songs."

On one occasion, which I mention not for its own sake, but for that of the contrasted occasion which I shall go on to relate, James Isaac happened to recollect the name of a ballad which he had been wont to sing before his habit of life had changed. The ballad was entitled "Glengyle," and the old man, with a painful effort of memory, quoted a stanza or two and a few disconnected lines. It was, as he assured me in his unimpassioned way, "a very good song, and set to very nice music."

A week or two later, when I was spending a busy afternoon in the company of old Bob, I mentioned this ballad and quoted a few lines that James Isaac had remembered. "Ah yes," said Bob sadly, "I mind of "Glengyle" well enough. But I don't know whether I can sing it for ye or not. I git so mad an' sorry every time I think o' that sneak of a Glengyle that it's jist as much as I can do to go on singin'. If ye're anxious to hear it, though, I'll see what I can do."

I protested, weakly, against any needless laceration of Bob's feelings, but he had already closed his eyes and knotted his brows. "I'll start it for ye, anyhow," he announced hastily, and the roar of the opening stanzas immediately followed:

> In yonder isle beyond Argyle,
>   Where flocks and herds were plenty,
> Lived a rich squire whose sister fair
>   Was the flower of all that country.
>
> The knight Sir Neil had wooed her long,
>   Expecting soon to marry.
> A highland laird his suit preferred,
>   Young, handsome, brisk, and airy.

Long she respected brave Sir Neil
  Because he wooed sincerely,
But as soon as she saw the young Glengyle
  He won her most entirely.

Till some lies to her brother came,
  That Neil had boasted proudly
Of favors from that lady young,
  Which made him vow thus rudely:

"I swear by all our friendships past,
  This hour again next morning
This knight or me shall lose our lives.
  He shall know who he's scorning."

Thus the tragic train of events is set in motion. Sir Neil, the most generous man and the best swordsman in all Scotland, is forced against his will to fight with the brother of his sweetheart, whom he kills in spite of his efforts merely to disarm him. Then the treacherous Glengyle comes upon the scene, taunts Sir Neil, and dares him to a second duel. Sir Neil protests vigorously against the necessity of killing all his friends in single combat, and

While talking thus he quit his guard.
  Glengyle in haste advancèd,
And pierced his generous, manly heart.
  The sword right through him glancèd.

The ballad was suddenly interrupted at this point by a howl of rage from the singer. "O God!" shouted Bob, "why aint I standin' right behind that Glengyle with a sword in me hand? Wouldn't I drive it through he's treacherous body!"

The ballad was ultimately finished, but not until Bob's grief and anger were partly assuaged by an imaginary torture and demolition of the scoundrelly Glengyle. Of small concern was it to Bob that he was singing "a good song, set to very nice music." The tragic tale of misunderstanding, treachery, and murder was to him a true report of human relationships in which, by virtue of his function as relater, he was constrained to bear a vicarious part.

Now that old Bob is upon the stage again for the moment he may be employed for the additional function of introducing, in a general way, his fellow-actors of French extraction who have played so important a part in the task of keeping ballads alive during these latter days. It will have been noticed that the recurrent name in these pages is Langille, and I should say that fully three-fourths of the ballads in my collection have been procured from singers answering to this name or to one equally Gallic in its origin. It must not be supposed, of course, that the Nova Scotians of French extraction continue with one consent to entertain their friends with old English and Scotch popular ballads, in blissful indifference to the fact that we have entered upon a new era of civilization. There are only a few old men and women, even of this race, who are thus minded to proclaim their affinities with the past; but, with the aid of these survivors, ballad-lore has lingered with the French a full generation after it was completely sloughed off by the Scotch people with whom they were associated in the same general community. To account for this fact I shall have to give a brief sketch of the French migrations to northern Nova Scotia.

This district was settled during the latter half of the

eighteenth century by Scotch immigrants. A large number of these people took up lands in the mountainous regions twenty or thirty miles inland, while others settled on the sea-coast or on the shores of the harbors and rivers with which this coast is plentifully indented; and the choice of settlement was, as I believe it always is, largely decided by the antecedent situation of the settler in the fatherland, since one who has lived among mountains in the parent country will naturally look for mountains when he comes to a new land, and one who has been reared within sight and sound of the ocean will still desire a daily assurance of the same inscrutable presence. These Nova Scotian settlements were, for some time, purely Scotch; but in the first quarter of the nineteenth century a new element appeared in the shape of a body of French Huguenots, who, after various rather obscure vicissitudes, had finally decided to put the ocean between themselves and the land which had proved so unnatural a home. They, for the most part, chose to settle among the Scotch people who were dwelling along or near the sea-coast.

The antecedents of these people will, I suppose, always remain a comparative mystery. They sternly repudiate the name of French, and insist on being regarded as Swiss. As I have many excellent reasons for wishing to maintain friendly relations with them I sometimes make a point of referring casually to their Swiss ancestry; and upon one occasion I was rewarded with a solution of the puzzle. This was given to me by an old man of the third generation from the first settlers.

"De old folks," he explained, "was livin' in France at de time, and Bonyparte made known to dem dat dey must jine Rome, leave de country, or die. Dey would not jine

Rome, an' dey was onwillin' to die, so dey left de country and made dere way to Switzerland, an' when dey crossed over to Nova Scotia dey crossed from Switzerland, an' dey was den Swiss people."

I have received, from other representatives of this transmuted stock, various hints which indicate the same general attitude towards the situation. But whether this was the exact state of the case or not it is at least certain that when they came to their new home across the Atlantic they came with no love for France graven upon their hearts. If they had any legends or customs taken from French soil they made no effort to retain them. Their language, at the time of their arrival in Nova Scotia, was a patois of French, but as soon as they conveniently could they dropped this in favor of the speech of their new neighbors. The children of the third generation, now old men and women, are loyal subjects of Great Britain. They speak with fervor of the mighty generalship of Wellington at the Battle of Waterloo, where, according to one of their versions which I have already presented from the point of view of Little Ned Langille, the victory was won through the prowess of "de Scotch Greys." They have legends, also, of Wolfe's great stroke in the conquest of Canada, and it was one of their most eloquent narrators that delivered the glowing exordium to his account of the battle: "Gineral Wolfe climbed de trecipice, camped on de Plains of Abraham, an' prayed for night or Blucher to come."

The French settlers, then, as we may agree to call them, lost no time in dropping their own language and customs and in adopting those of their new neighbors; and, as they were passionately fond of music, one of the most important of their new acquisitions was that of the popular

ballads in vogue among those neighbors. This process
was accomplished, not by the sturdy farmers and God-
fearing citizens who formed the more prosperous element
of the new race, but by the merrier and more carnal-
minded ones who were employed in great numbers by the
Scotch as housemaids and farm-hands. A very natural
result followed. The Scotch people gradually abandoned
a practice that was becoming one of the chief pastimes of
their servants.

Speaking very roughly, then, one may say this. The
second generation of the French settlers monopolized the
English and Scotch ballads in vogue among their neighbors and passed them on to the third generation, the members of which continued to sing them with unabated zeal;
but when the children of the fourth generation arrived at
years of conventional discretion they fell in with the spirit
of the new times and began to suspect that ballad-singing
was one of the simple pastimes of a ruder age. By far the
greater number of the ballads in my collection have been
procured from men and women of the third generation, of
whom there are still a few survivors ranging from seventy-
five to ninety years of age.

This general statement has received its illustration in
many of the individual cases that I have discussed in the
preceding chapters, where the French name Langille figures so largely. The nomen Langille includes many
branches or families in the north shore counties of Pictou
and Colchester, and it was represented, a few years back,
by such notable personages as Bob and Little Ned, who
lived in villages separated by several miles and who were
unaware of each other's existence. But the most important person of the name, from the point of view of the

present discussion, is Edward the father of Little Ned and the son of one of the original settlers. Old Edward was gathered to his fathers long before my recollection, but I have heard much concerning him from his children. He looms heroically in my imagination as the mighty bard who "could sing all day for ye an' never sing the same song twict," and it is a fact to be recorded without further comment that he bore so marked a resemblance to another of the great figures of the past that he was known in the community as "old Napoleon." This great man, according to the account given by his children, spent his youth in the employ of a Scotch family, where he proceeded in victorious fashion to annex and appropriate a long list of English and Scottish popular ballads.

It would be possible to go on heaping up instances of this transference of a body of folk-lore to the members of an alien race, but I have probably said enough to fix the impression which I have given in scattered fashion throughout the preceding chapters, and I may therefore proceed to the third cause of the decline and fall of ballad-singing in my particular district. The first two causes that I have assigned in this chapter—namely, the superseding of the ballads by more modern songs and the abandoning of them by a superior and disdainful race—have been kept pretty constantly before the reader; but the destructive force that I am now to consider, namely, disapproval of ballad-singing from religious motives, I have had occasion to suggest only in one or two instances.

Three summers ago I spent some time in canvassing the Scotch communities in the interior of the northern counties, but without success. Everywhere I found testimony to the fact that ballads had been sung in the past, and it will be remembered that old James Isaac Macdonald's home at the West River, which is one of the communities under discussion, literally teemed with ballads in the bygone days of his youth. Many of the persons in this part of the country, seeing in me a brother Scot, were inclined to regard me with friendliness and confidence, and I had every opportunity of discovering ballads if there had been any to discover. I have just been speaking of the fact that the Scotch people nearer the sea-coast had given up ballad-singing when they found that they were sharing the pastime with a lower order of beings; but this explanation will not cover the case of the inland districts, where there are practically no people of French descent, or of any descent except Scotch.

The earlier settlers in these districts were not a very sober or God-fearing people. They had no ministers and no religious services during the first years of their settlement, and they were, on the whole, much more inclined to the pleasures of the fiddle and the rum-keg than to the more sober comforts of religion. An admirable account of these early settlers is given by the late Rev. George Patterson, in his "History of the County of Pictou," and I shall quote from his book a brief passage in which he himself is quoting from the diary of Dr. McGregor, the first minister who appeared in that part of the country. Dr. McGregor was sent out, in 1786, by the Synod of Scotland, and his first religious service, which was held "in Squire Patterson's barn," he thus describes:

The Squire gave orders to lay slabs and planks in his barn for seats to the congregation; and before eleven o'clock next morning I saw the people gathering to hear the Gospel from the lips of a stranger who felt few of its consolations, and had but little hope of communicating them to his hearers. None came by land except certain families who lived a few miles to the right and left of Squire Patterson's. Those who came from the south side of the harbour and from the river had to come in boats and canoes containing from one to seven or eight persons. The congregation, however, was not large; for numbers could not get ready their craft, the notice was so short. I observed that the conduct of some of them, coming from the shore to the barn, was as if they had never heard of a Sabbath. I heard loud talking and laughing, and singing and whistling even before they reached the shore. They behaved, however, with decency so long as I continued to speak, and some of them were evidently much affected. I endeavoured to explain to them in the forenoon in English, "This is a faithful saying and worthy of all acceptation, that Christ Jesus came into the world to save sinners," and in the afternoon, in Gaelic, "The Son of Man is come to seek and to save that which is lost." The first words which I heard, after pronouncing the blessing, were from a gentleman of the army calling to his companions, "Come, come, let us go to the grog shop"; but instead of going with him, they came toward me to bid me welcome to the settlement, and he came himself at last.

From a regenerate point of view this is a gloomy picture, relieved only at the close by a glimpse of that hospitality which is the instinct of every Scotchman whether he be citizen or outlaw. But as for me I have a wholly unregenerate longing to know what songs these impious Scots were chanting to the swing of the paddle and the oar as they came down the river on that violated Sabbath morning a hundred and thirty years ago. The Scriptural lore which they were to receive is without variableness or shadow of turning, but the "loud talking and laughing and whistling and singing" were soon to give place to a godly solemnity and decorum, and the place which knew the ancient folk-lore of Scotland was to know it no more.

These early settlers had goodly store of ballads with them when they came from Scotland, and new arrivals were continually bringing new specimens and fresh versions, so that it may be seen that ballad-singing had its day among these exiles who were clinging passionately to the customs and diversions which reminded them of their lost motherland. But, as fortunately, perhaps, for the eternal welfare of their immortal souls as it is unfortunate for the purposes of our study, they were presently brought under the influence of a zealous band of ministers who came from Scotland in increasing numbers as the nineteenth century proceeded, and who set themselves ardently to the task of converting these heathen from the error of their ways. Now, as we all know, a converted Scotchman has no dealings with the merrier aspects of life. He may "take a wee drap" occasionally "for the stomach's sake"—a purely serious proceeding, to be regarded as a necessary precaution against illness—but the singing of light and immodest songs can have no place in his scheme of things. It cannot help the body, and it imperils the immortal soul. Therefore, as religion advanced ballad-singing receded, and it was resigned the more easily in that its place was being filled by the noble music and stirring words of the paraphrases and the Psalms of David.

In many parts of the country I have received good evidence of this supplanting of the ballads. A thoroughly typical case is that of a farmer named William McKay, whom I have known for many years. He lives in one of these inland Scotch communities, and he has aided me in fixing several of the impressions that I have been discussing. His father, now long deceased, was once possessed of a varied assortment of Scotch ballads which he sang freely and merrily during William's own childhood; but presently he became a "professor" of religion, and then he completely renounced his ballads and sternly forebade his children ever to pollute their mouths with these profane and godless songs. My friend had himself learned a few of these songs before the fountains of secular music had become dry, but all that he has ever been able to recollect for me is a stanza or two from "Our Goodman." He is about fifty years old, and is a merry, companionable person who has gone out into the world at times and completely sloughed off the fanaticism bequeathed by his father, therefore he would have had no sort of objection to singing the ballads he once knew—if he could only have remembered them. But they had been denied him so long that at length they had passed from his possession forever.

I have now outlined what I believe to be the three main reasons for the almost complete disappearance of popular ballads in a country that was once rich in possibilities for the collector. Unhappily there was no collector to enrich himself with these almost boundless possibilities, and the scheme of things has allowed me only a belated appearance on the scene, with the opportunity of gathering some scattered fragments and the doubtful privilege of inquiring into the various causes which have conspired, under the leadership of Civilization, to bring about the present depleted condition of folk-lore.

Gramley Library
Salem College
Winston-Salem, NC 27108